CHRISTINE SANDMAN

THE MODERN MANAGEMENT MENTOR

NEXT-LEVEL TOOLS FOR NEW MANAGERS

ISBN 13: 978-1-63489-631-3
Library of Congress Catalog Number has been applied for.
Printed in the United States of America
First Printing: 2023
28 27 26 25 24   6 5 4 3 2

Design by Cindy Samargia Laun

Wise Ink
PO Box 580195
Minneapolis, MN 55458-0195
WiseInk.com

Wise Ink is a creative publishing agency for game-changers. Wise Ink authors uplift, inspire, and inform,
and their titles support building a better and more equitable world.
For more information, visit WiseInk.com.

To order, visit ItascaBooks.com ChristineSandmanStone.com. Reseller discounts available.

Contact Christine Sandman Stone at ChristineSandmanStone.com for speaking engagements, freelance
writing projects, and interviews.

CONTENTS

FOREWORD

Are you a newly minted leader looking for solid, on-the-ground advice on how to lead? Wish you had a wise older sister to coach you? Christine was that mentor for me. Back in 2016, as a young start-up CEO, I experienced one of the hardest years of my life: we were running out of money, team dynamics were filled with strain and frustration, and worst of all, my cofounder and I weren't on speaking terms. I knew instinctively that it was a leadership issue, and since I was that leader, the change had to come from me. Fortunately, Christine became the mentor I sorely needed at that time, and she helped me construct better frameworks for communication and filled in my leadership gaps with constructive, specific advice. Now the company is in a much better place.

So, you're in good hands, just as I was! This pragmatic book is your best friend—it's full of the practical and nitty-gritty. You are about to embark on a meaningful journey that will find you in difficult conversations, between rocks and hard places, and ensconced in the fulfilling discipline of leading people. And that's the best part: people! Parts of this will be discovering yourself; the other parts will be gathering the tools in your leadership "toolbox."

Leadership truly is a discipline—it can be learned, it can be practiced, and anyone can become great at it. When I was a combat platoon leader in the US Army, learning to lead was a vital part of my duty, my identity, and my calling. Leaders are not born; they learn and rise to the challenge. It is not a mysterious cloud of charisma surrounding a few; it is a principled calling with an associated set of skills to influence, support, and direct. And, like any other human endeavor, it has a body of knowledge passed down through generations and cultivated as a shared, living trust of expertise. This book encapsulates much of that knowledge in a detailed, substantive way. Christine and Madeline have distilled their hard-earned knowledge into a handy resource to help the new manager navigate key moments of leadership.

And the beauty of it is that it only grows: what Christine passed down to me, I can pass to others, and so shall you. We all become leaders at some point—sharing and supporting each other, organizing ourselves to row toward common goals.

So, wherever you are in your leadership journey, you have come to the right place. Enjoy the journey and dive right in!

— *Kimberly Jung, former US Army engineer officer and OEF veteran,*
CEO of Blanchard House, former CEO of Rumi Spice,
Successful Shark Tank Entepreneur,
investor, teammate

GRATITUDE

Over the course of a life, we collect funny stories, joyous moments of achievements, and memories. Sometimes we collect rocks, bar coasters, Vans tennis shoes, and other things that become precious to us. I have been collecting badasses: great leaders, entrepreneurs, advocates. These are the badasses who were central to this project:

Madeline Stone Kutis, your personal problem statement of searching for resources for first-time people managers was the catalyst for this project. You are a joyous, articulate, hard-driving collaborator.

E. T. Stone, your work as a writing coach to smart undergrads is a gift to me. Your challenge to build out stories brought those stories to life. Your positive response to editing changes and the hours you spent on this were greatly appreciated. Can't wait to read your dissertation.

Claire Eliot Stone, you have a lens that helps you catch things others miss, and you are my tether to make sure concepts are complete. Your thorough consideration of ideas is a remarkable asset.

Lauren Henry, you took this book to the UK and piloted the earliest copy. Your thoughts were essential for one of the early pivots.

To my early readers, thanks so much for reacting and letting me know what worked well and how to bring more of that into the work.

Kimberly Jung, your ability to put counsel into action drives your success. I love our conversations; thank you for your support of this project.

Megan McCann, Leslie Vickery, and Jane Hamner, thank you for starting ARA (Attract, Retain, Advance Women in Tech). You have connected me with so many remarkable women leaders. You actively, materially elevate others. I'm grateful to be in your circle.

To the leaders I worked with whose best practices I admire: Deb Hall-Lefevre, Ed Dzadovsky, Machelle Williams, Carol Davis Ives, John Higginson, Kristy Braden, Amanda Lannert, Gary Sheaffer, Sandee Kastrul, Tiara Wheatley, and others.

Chicago Innovation Awards Women's Mentoring Co-op, thank you to the remarkable mentors and mentees who create one of my favorite vibrant communities, and thanks to Luke Tanen for his continued support of this critical co-op that elevates women and supports innovation in Chicago.

Katie Dowling, I appreciate your deep insight on Agile transformation and on humans, in general. So grateful we connected years ago.

Jack Sandman, thank you for being a great dad and role model of a leader who paid attention and deliberately changed to get better.

To Wise Ink: Dara and the team, you walk your talk, elevating voices and ideas. You are an asset to me and so many others. Kate, your developmental edit showed me why your authors and corporate clients both deeply appreciate your gifts. Hanna, your energy and insight helped set strategy.

Henry Stone, I appreciate the shrimp pasta, risotto, and other great food provided on writing workshop weekends. Thanks for asking hard questions; it makes the answers stronger.

And lastly, to Jim Stone. Thank you for your love, helping me laugh, helping me leap. You are my best decision.

ORIGIN STORY

When my oldest offspring, Madeline Stone Kutis, started working as a people manager for the first time, she reached out to ask for help. I've managed teams for twenty-plus years at start-up and large companies and studied organizational development in my graduate work. I have a deep fascination with team dynamics and performance. She knew not only would I help, but I kind of nerd out on this kind of work.

If I set my parental biases aside about Madeline's talents, I can still confirm she is a highly successful product and program manager in the tech companies she works for. She asks the hard questions others don't ask, she delivers projects that others struggle with, and she has clear vision and outcomes for the products she owns. If you have a dictionary with type A/straight A student definition, I am sure she is referenced there.

When she became a first-time manager, she wanted to get great grades in that too. At times she doubted herself (I think she was the only one), and she asked me to be her mentor.

As Madeline and I talked, I shared lists of questions I would ask in one-on-one meetings and guidance about how a manager can figure out a new company or team. We would dive into challenges she was having with performance, making adjustments, or measuring results. I would share solutions that worked for me in the past (sometimes a few different ones). She would use the tools, and then reflect and give me her reactions. Sometimes things worked well; sometimes we could tell the tool needed to be adjusted to be effective for her.

She's tough and smart and unafraid. This process of working together helped refine and develop the tool you have today.

Our voices—mine from years of experience and hers from recent, authentic application and implementation of the ideas—come together to give you the chance to accelerate and excel as a manager.

The Challenge

As Madeline and I started our conversations, we realized her struggles were far from unique. Many of us have seen a scene like this:

The auditorium buzzed with conversation. Seats were packed, and people moved up and down aisles, hoping their friends had held spots for them. The front row, usually empty, was completely full. Communications folks ran around making sure feeds were live to regional and global locations. Everyone was there to see the new CEO.

It was his first week and first all-company meeting. Everyone was energized; this person had been very successful in an international division of the company. He was a strong presence and an engaging public speaker. The energy in the room was like the moments before a sold-out concert begins.

As he walked onto the auditorium stage, everyone spontaneously applauded. He spoke decisively, sharing that he believed everyone in the room and on the call was needed to turn the company around. Teams would lead with innovation, ask hard questions, and drive growth from within. The company would rise like a phoenix, and journalists would write of the recovery in

Harvard Business Review and Forbes. When the meeting concluded, everyone was cheering, smiling, and talking energetically.

That day, people returned to their teams and in the weeks that followed, they did their work, but nothing changed. "Lead with innovation!" was an exciting message that made sense during the high-energy meeting, but no one knew how to change decisions, work, behavior, teams, and approach to start innovating. The CEO didn't take the next step to define areas where they would innovate, the way he would seek feedback and insight and answer hard questions, what the teams should work on (and not work on), and how the company would measure progress.

He gave them words of inspiration, but hadn't taken the steps to help teams understand how they would change their work approach to get those results. They didn't have the bridge of explanation between his words and their daily work, especially a clear sense of practical things each of them could do, and each of the teams could do. The company declined, and he was replaced.

This challenge isn't just one that C-level executives face. This lack of practical guidance happens at the manager level, too, and this level is even more critical. When you're starting as a first-time manager, you can be especially vulnerable to feeling energized by big ideas and become paralyzed or overwhelmed when it's time to implement them.

That was what happened to Charlotte, an excellent individual contributor who was promoted to a management position within her company. Her manager believed in her and supported Charlotte's development by sending her to a series of classes in first-time manager leadership development. She heard great ideas on giving feedback in the moment and building relationships with her peers. Her head was full of thoughts and hopes. She left class on an energy high, but returned to a failing project and a team in crisis. She focused on the crisis, her classes forgotten. A year later, Charlotte left the firm to take an individual contributor role as a data architect.

Business books and tech leaders talk about concepts at a high level (setting goals, transparency, autonomy, innovation, talent development, and talent pipeline), but many cannot give their staff pragmatic ways to achieve these things. Staff, such as Charlotte, walk away from leadership conversations, training, and presentations energized by the ideas, but deflate when they aren't sure what they can do about them. A business analyst or product specialist might think, "I am glad I work for a company that is aspiring to own our market, but that doesn't change my daily work. That's for higher-level people to deliver."

The truth is, execution has to happen at all levels for significant change to occur. Ultimately, all staff need simple, specific, actionable translation and practical guidance to enact change. It's like a screenplay. There are stage directions in clear language by actor, definition of the sets and settings, and director notes with the lines actors deliver. It's an everyday guide, and each actor chooses the part of the screenplay they need to succeed for their day. Each of the teams (cinematography, stunts, makeup, costumes, casting) use this clear guide to deliver. It has simple, straightforward tasks to promote success.

There is significant value gained when inspirational leadership and company vision translate into practical actions and results for teams; there are other benefits for companies and workers that were considered when writing this everyday management guide.

First, diversity. Fewer women and people of color are in management roles, and reports have called this the "broken rung" of the career ladder.[1] Inexperienced, yet high-potential managers are out there. If we can help them build practical ways to lead, the opportunity is significant for both companies and the workforce.

A 2021 study found that gender-diverse teams financially outperform non-diverse teams by 25 percent, and ethnically diverse teams outperform non-diverse teams by 36 percent.[2]

What CEO wouldn't give a body part for a 25 to 36 percent improvement in performance?

Second, employee engagement. When employees have a strong mental and emotional connection to their places of work, they are more engaged and energized. If we look at engagement, which is harder to assess, there is great research about how feeling included is a critical part of engagement. Being the only woman, LGBTQ+ person, or person of color on a team leads to feelings of exclusion and lowers engagement. Why does engagement matter? According to Gallup, highly engaged teams are 23 percent more productive and profitable.[3]

These are HUGE numbers that should command companies' attention. As we are writing this book in 2022, businesses are in a resourcing crisis, but the solution is really right in front of them, in the form of building and nurturing diverse, engaged teams.

This book provides practical, tested tools for new managers. Management is not a talent you are born with—it is a skill that can be taught and learned, and you can become an expert. My mentoring conversations with Madeline unfolded over a year, and this book includes the tools I shared, she used, she reflected on, and we adapted.

About Christine

I was an accidental technologist more than 30 years ago. I started my career writing technical documentation in a small tech company and fell in love with it. My career roles progressed from working as a data center architect to running projects, then larger projects, then rescuing other managers' projects that were in crisis, writing best practices and teaching others. I naturally progressed into leading teams and large change efforts in technical companies, including Agile development transformations, global execution of Objectives and Key Results (OKRs), and strategic planning. In the middle of my career, I went back to school and earned my master's in organizational development. It was the perfect time to immerse myself in the study of human change and performance. I have worked with great bosses, led great teams, experienced great stories, and have an authentic joy for my work.

At four large companies (Dell, McDonald's, Volkswagen, and Groupon), I have built teams and led change. More importantly, the changes I built outlasted my time at these companies.

1 McKinsey, *Women in the Workplace 2021*, September 27, 2021, https://www.mckinsey.com/-/media/ mckinsey/featured%20insights/diversity%20and%20inclusion/women%20in%20the%20workplace%202021/ women-in-the-workplace-2021.pdf.

2 McKinsey, Exhibit 1, *Diversity Wins: How Inclusion Matters*, May 19, 2020, https://www.mckinsey.com/ featured-insights/diversity-and-inclusion/diversity-wins-how-inclusion-matters.

3 Gallup, *State of the Global Workplace: 2022 Report*, https://www.gallup.com/workplace/349484/state-of- the-global-workplace-2022-report.aspx.

One of my core strengths is breaking high-level goals and visions into objectives and actions that help large teams do work and achieve results in better ways. Even when I am creating an $80 million turnaround plan to reform the work of more than a thousand technologists, I keep things as simple as possible, focusing on the fastest path to success. Things I have learned from my remarkable employers and bosses are woven into how I lead and deliver:

- **From Dell: the power of quarterly goals and measurement.** Setting objectives every 90 days taught me the deep value of thoughtful action plans, measured and rewritten every quarter. This practice supported a critical team turnaround.
- **From McDonald's: the importance of telling the story so everyone can execute without checking with leadership.** I worked alongside a remarkable Change Management team at McDonald's. They taught me to understand the impact business pivots have on people, and how critical it was to clarify everyone's path and objectives. They would create a clear, common language and phrases for everyone to use. One year was dubbed "The Year of the Drive Thru," and we knew our main goal for the year was to speed service in that part of restaurant operations.
- **From Volkswagen/Audi: how empathy and understanding people are critical to getting the best from teams.** We used tools like Myers-Briggs Type Indicator, Insights Discovery, and The Whole Brain Model, and spent time understanding their implications. The Organizational Effectiveness team at Volkswagen/Audi taught managers how to use these tools to build and strengthen teams.
- **From Groupon: the power of Objectives and Key Results as a tool to lead large-scale execution.** OKRs involve pairing a business goal (objective) with a key result (quantitative measurement of outcome) and aligning your work to support those. This method forces decision-making, prioritization, and measurement of both success and failure. Our Agile software development transformation achieved exceptional results when we tied technical work tightly to OKRs. The scale of transparency and decision-making was critical to surviving the pandemic in 2020 and 2021.

In addition to my own teams, I mentor people managers and leaders in large companies like Google, Amazon, Microsoft, Etsy, Grubhub, IBM, and Zillow; in tech start-ups like Ballentine, Handshake, Jellyvision, Reverb, and Tempus; and in other organizations in the nonprofit sector. Because I believe in measuring results, I keep running lists of people I coach to promotions and new opportunities. My exposure to many organizations and the continued success of these remarkable people I work with confirms this:

Anyone can manage and lead. It is a learned, reinforced skill set.

Welcome

Being a great manager can be learned.

Strong managers learn all the time and keep getting better, especially as their responsibilities grow.

This book is meant to accelerate your success as a first-time people manager by helping you learn faster and giving you an everyday guide.

Because you are reading this, I know you are:

1. Curious
2. Interested in doing well
3. Facing a new challenge

You already have what it takes to thrive as a manager—you are interested and ready to work. The best part about your orientation toward growth is that it will help you AND your team.

This guide was written from two different perspectives. As a senior tech leader, I came into this project with decades of experience and a menu of tools and methods. As a first-time people manager, my daughter, Madeline, approached this project with fresh eyes and current lived experience. I wrote the guide, and she provided valuable insights. As we worked together, we kept track of what worked well, made adjustments, and learned collectively.

You can reach us at www.modernmanagementmentor.com with your questions.

Madeline and I have your back.

You've got this.

HOW TO USE THIS GUIDE

This book is designed to give you what you need when you need it. It's like a field guide, or screenplay. Move to the section for your need and situation—the insights and how-to guides will provide relevant information to you when you need it.

Many manager roles open when there is a problem on the team. And even if there isn't a problem, you are coming into a manager role that was previously held by someone else. So, the team is used to a familiar way of working, established processes (whether functional or dysfunctional), and relationships with other teams and partners.

During her first week as a people manager, Madeline had to deal with a significant team problem that involved both human and technical issues. We designed our approach to help her (and you) get what is needed when it is needed. This book is designed to be simple and practical.

To get the most out of this book, we suggest the following three approaches:

1. **Be opportunistic.** Give each section a quick glance and jump to the one that helps you right now. Skip around as needed.

2. **Carry this book with you.** It can guide you on specific actions, questions to ask others, or topics to consider when you have some downtime.

3. **Look at the suggested worksheets and adapt them** for yourself and your particular circumstances. Use the questions that work for you and the tools that will help you most. When you use the worksheets, use whichever medium that is best for you. Perhaps you prefer an online program for note-taking? Or love traditional paper notebooks? Or use a notes app on your phone?

When I showed up for my first week at Dell, they shared a slide that showed the ranking of teams in the United States. Mine was ranked 33rd of 33. We were performing poorly in every category: lowest customer satisfaction, most late projects, most projects over budget, highest technical defects. It was an intense (and ultimately successful) few years. Had someone given me this book, I would have cried at first. How the heck was I going to do all these things? How could I get to know my team, my peers, my boss, our work, and the strategy? How could I improve our situation, promote growth, and measure progress? The methods that appear in this book are the very ones that saved me and elevated my team.

Fit reading and workbook activities into your calendar whenever you have time. As you work your way through this book, we hope you can sense us on the sidelines saying, "You've got this."

Start Strong

No matter what issues are going on in your job, your very first and most important goal is to establish a positive relationship with your boss. And, as the saying goes, "Don't f*ck it up" with everyone else. :)

FIRST DAYS

⟳ Goal: Don't mess up

A great start sets the tone. During your first weeks, you have two goals:

1. Build your relationship with your boss
2. Don't mess up

In the first week, Job One is to focus on starting positively, especially with your boss and team. Most important to your success is your relationship with your boss. Start with a conversation to collect information. Whenever you check in during the first weeks, pay attention to building rapport.

For everyone else, your goal is to make a positive first impression and not mess up. Don't do stupid stuff early on! You will set yourself back if you try to get ahead too quickly or commit a workplace faux pas. If you have been promoted within the same company, think of first impressions as "first impressions as a manager." You're in a different role now, so people will start to see you in a different way. If you are unhappy with some aspect of your personal brand, now is the time for a fresh start.

You can get in your own way by making mistakes. The most common mistakes first-time managers make are these:

1. **Arrogance**
   When someone who used to be a top project manager is now in charge of other project managers, that person can make the mistake of communicating that their own personal best practices are better than others' approaches. Before you hurry to share your wisdom, stop and listen closely. It could be that someone on your team has an idea that is actually better for their situation. Quick diagnoses based on early information can lead to mistakes and people thinking you are a jerk.

2. **Familiarity**
   Pressure comes with being a manager, and some social norms have higher stakes. I am known for peppering my conversations creatively with curse words, but when meeting with a group, I rein in my language. I have inadvertently offended others with my careless colorful language.

3. **Impatience**
   You will feel an urgency to lead, and you might communicate that to your team. You also may be inclined to jump in and do others' work for them. Resist that inclination. It takes time to slow down, observe, and make learning your top priority. Be pleasant, kind, and neutral. Someone you overlook in the first weeks can end up being your go-to person weeks later. Give yourself time to understand people and work.

It's hard work to be cautious, neutral, and actively listen to many people to understand the full picture. In addition to avoiding the pitfalls listed above, it's important to do the simple things too: be on time, dress to the norms of your company, and stay out of gossip. Striving to not make these mistakes during those first few weeks will help you build a positive image and first impression with others.

How people see you (your "personal brand") changes how they treat you and your team. Your brand is being built every moment you ask a question, join a meeting, or have a conversation. How you react when faced with a problem will give people a lasting impression of how you react to conflict. How you respond to your mistakes will give your team an expectation of how you are likely to treat them if they make an error. Your humility and orientation to learning will build trust with others and demonstrate you are interested in their success, not just your own. When you celebrate an accomplishment, people will make assumptions about your values and expectations.

Ultimately, your brand will be part of how others decide to collaborate with you, support you, and give you future opportunities. Don't panic! You were hired for a reason. The people interviewing you liked you, and you likely had some kind of rapport with them. Be your marvelous self and, if you'd like to learn more about building a personal brand, skip ahead to page 29.

Keep in mind that the factors that made you a successful individual contributor are different from what will brand you a successful people manager. Strong leaders have a learning mindset, authenticity, a sincere interest in others and the company culture, approachability, and humility.

FIRST MEETING WITH YOUR BOSS

⊃ **Goal: Invest in this most important relationship early**

Usually, your new boss will set up a meeting close to your start date. If not, reach out and schedule one. Here are great questions to ask during that meeting and the reasons behind them:

Who is valuable to talk to/build relationships with?

Take notes, then work the list. Once your boss gives you the names and explains why these folks are important, you can reach out on your own when you have time.

Send an email structured something like this:

Chris, Jocy mentioned you are her go-to person for questions about marketing...
Or: *Ellen, Jocy mentioned you have great insight about our new vertical...*

Sending these emails is beneficial because:

1. They show interest and respect for wise people in the organization. This kind of request is flattering and is a great way to start a working relationship.
2. They show respect for your boss's insight.
3. You can do this on your own time/schedule. Got a light day? Schedule three conversations. Got a few busy days? Schedule your conversations for next week.

How do you prefer I communicate with you when I have a question or update (face-to-face, email, etc.)?

This is critical because someone might say, "Actually, messages are great. If I get busy, I can reply later in the day." Or they might say, "Please just drop by my office. I'd much rather connect in person during your first month."

Ask. People are more likely to give you their best when they are in their comfort zone. And you might be surprised by how strong others' personal communication preferences are.

What is the best way for me to escalate an issue?

This seems similar to the question above, but it is very different. Here you are asking how to best reach out if there is an issue of urgency. Should you use instant messaging? Email? Text? The previous question addresses how best to update your boss or ask informational questions. This question focuses on reaching your boss quickly for an emergency. Asking this question shows you understand the difference. Oftentimes, managers will have different answers. Perhaps the manager who prefers to see you face-to-face for standard questions prefers a text when there is a crisis so they see it right away.

What is the biggest problem for me to solve? And how will we measure progress?

Here you are asking: "What is the most pressing problem you need me to solve quickly?" You are looking for guidance on what needs to happen first, and you need an understanding of why it is urgent. Sometimes there isn't a problem to solve. In other cases, there is, and it is critical you know what work to prioritize. Ask follow-up questions to make sure you understand the problem to solve and how you and your boss will know when it is better. Follow up with written notes and next steps so you can confirm your understanding of the problem that needs immediate attention.

What is the current strength of the team?

This question gives you insight on the best and fastest way to build on the team's results. If you understand where the team thrives and drives results, you can try to amplify those strengths to improve outcomes.

What is the biggest gain you want me to make with the team?

Here you are asking how the team might be expected to grow in capacity. A different way to ask this is, "What struggles or obstacles are preventing the team from delivering work effectively?" Usually this is not connected to the biggest business problem to solve, instead to the ways in which the team gets work done. Most teams have challenges, as well as goals.

Are there key meetings I should put on my calendar? (And does my team already have a cadence for meetings that I should continue?)

This question helps you understand commitments you will need to build into your calendar, both as a member of your boss's leadership group, and with your own team. It's interesting to see if you hear any recommendations for change or adjustment when you ask this question.

Are there HR guidelines or training I should familiarize myself with as a people manager?

This guide isn't meant to cover labor laws or legal liabilities. Make sure you are familiar with your company, state, and Human Resources expectations.

Is there anything I can do for you?

This question is important. It shows you understand your role as a support person to your boss AND it opens the door for the manager to ask you for something unexpected. I have had new opportunities come to me from this question. In one case, my boss's request to set up a team meeting with the CEO led to an opportunity to meet and converse with the company CEO for the first time.

May I have 15 minutes on your calendar at the end of the day during this first week or two?

This gives you a chance to pose any questions and share progress from the day. You may mention, "I met with Bob today to talk about strategy," and your boss might reply, "Oh gosh, not Bob. Actually, you need to talk to . . ." Or she might say, "Great, did he tell you about the upgrade?" (And if he didn't, you know to go back and chat further.)

This is an effective way to establish your autonomy and observe your boss's quick reactions. Save up questions you have collected during the day like, "I realized today I am not sure how we back up data here," or "Is there a supply of sticky notes I can use for my Agile board?"

Worksheet: Manager Expectations

Who is valuable to talk to/build relationships with?

NAME	ROLE	REASON TO CONNECT

What is the best way to communicate with you (face-to-face, email, other)?

What is the best way to escalate an urgent situation (Slack or Teams? Email? Text?)?

What is the biggest problem you'd like me to solve?

What is the best way to measure progress on solving this challenge?

What are the main strengths of the team?

What is the biggest gain for me to make with the team from a developmental perspective? (Or: What are ways you'd like to see the team grow next year?)

Are there key meetings I should put on my calendar?
(And does my team already have a cadence for meetings I should continue?)

Are there HR guidelines or training with which I should familiarize myself?

Are there any important operational events I have responsibilities for?
(For example, performance reviews, a big company meeting, etc.)

Is there anything I can do for you?

May I put 15 minutes on your calendar at the end of each day for this first week or two to check in?

Worksheet: First Week/s Running Questions List

It's helpful to keep a running list of questions and add to it every day. When you check in with your boss, go over things you have collected on this list—a person you want to know more about, a term you didn't understand, a practical question about scheduling an event, and so on. These first weeks present a unique opportunity to ask anything. Write down your note, and check it off when you get an answer. (To be honest, I continue this practice even after my first weeks. I keep track of updates or questions for my boss, which helps me have a constantly evolving and updated agenda for our one-on-ones.)

_____

_____

_____

_____

_____

_____

_____

_____

_____

_____

_____

_____

ONE-ON-ONES WITH YOUR BOSS

⊃ **Goal: Use a recurring, lightly structured connection to support your relationship**

After your first meeting, set up recurring one-on-one meetings with your boss. They should be:

- at least 30 minutes,
- weekly,
- and your boss should have the option to reschedule if needed.

Each time you meet, come prepared with items to discuss. Typical topics might include:

1. **Top priorities** for the week: Especially in your first months, this is a great way to confirm you have the most important areas of focus at the top of your list. Your boss might say, "Perfect!" Or she might say, "I am surprised I didn't see the security audit on here." It's very simple to adjust the list in the moment, and then you can go into your week confident you aren't missing something important.
2. **Questions** that have come up over the week: Urgent questions can be asked outside of this meeting so you have an immediate answer, but some can wait until you are face-to-face. This shows your boss you are actively learning and organized about following up.
3. **Heads ups:** Give your boss an early warning about things that might concern her in the future. No action is required—the purpose is simply awareness.
4. **My team/my people:** Make a point of calling out folks who are thriving, as well as folks who may be struggling.
5. **Escalations that require assistance:** Ask about priority items that will likely require her assistance or guidance.
6. **Decisions/FYIs (For Your Information):** Fill your boss in on any relevant progress.
7. **Work status:** Leave work status updates for last because your boss may already be aware what work is being accomplished. Don't make this a boring readout. In fact, it doesn't even need to be covered in detail unless your boss is interested.

If you can keep this meeting interactive and conversational, deliberately bringing in questions for her to answer, or guidance you need, it keeps the energy of the meeting productive.

This is a simple way to set a productive, collaborative tone and positive relationship with your boss.

2

Your Work Sponsor

(Though your company likely will call them a "mentor")

If you weren't assigned a mentor, ask for one. This person will likely become one of your first sponsors and advocates within the organization.

YOUR FIRST SPONSOR

⟳ **Goal: Find a sponsor in your first 90 days**

Usually, a new role comes with a "mentor." If not, ask for one. A great time to do this is in your first meetings with your boss, after your onboarding is complete. Ask if your boss can connect you with someone who would be a good advisor during your first months. Although you are really asking for a sponsor, most companies call these individuals mentors. It's critical to understand the difference.

Carla Harris, the only black woman to rise to Vice Chair at Morgan Stanley, once said that you should tell your mentor the good, the bad, and the ugly. You should tell your sponsor the good, the good, and the good.[1]

A sponsor is someone who will advocate for you to get more responsibilities, a promotion, a new opportunity. They need to see your successes, your talents. A mentor is someone to whom you can show self-doubt, frustration, failure. If a company-assigned mentor is part of your organization's career development support system, they might rate you as "not quite ready" for the next role, since they know about your struggles.

So, while this company-assigned person may be called a "mentor," treat them like a sponsor. Know that what they learn from you will likely be shared with others and may impact your future work assignments and promotions.

This person will be:

- A supplemental source of information
- An important support person
- An advocate for your future endeavors
- Responsible (usually) for helping you succeed in the team

P.S. Make sure you have someone to whom you CAN tell the good, the bad, and the ugly. This person should be outside of your company—a TRUE mentor. We all need that support too.

---

1 Hilary Burns, "The Mentor vs. the Sponsor: Who Gets to Hear the Good, the Bad and the Ugly?," *Bizwomen*, March 31, 2016, https://www.bizjournals.com/bizwomen/news/profiles-strategies/2014/11/the-mentor-vs-the-sponsor-who-gets-to-hear-the.html.

Hot tip!

HOW TO FIND A REAL "SAFE TO TALK ABOUT THE GOOD, THE BAD, AND THE UGLY" MENTOR

This section and the next worksheet focuses on your sponsor.

Ideally, you will have both a sponsor (your advocate in the company who will field questions and listen to your updates of positive progress) AND a mentor (someone to whom you can tell the good, the bad, and the ugly). Here are some suggestions for finding a mentor:

First: Start outside your company. Is there someone you know from a past job or company that you admired? Reach out to see if they would be willing to act as a guide.

Second: Look for mentoring organizations in your city.

Third: Browse your social network or networking groups for forums and new potential sources of support.

Lastly: If you need to look inside your company, wait until you find someone you can trust, ideally in another division or team.

Worksheet: Mentor (Sponsor) Conversation

I'd love to understand how you came to work here. What brought you to the company?

_____

_____

What keeps you here?

_____

_____

Can you give me an overview of your role and your areas of focus here?

_____

_____

Who do you believe thrives within the company?

_____

_____

Can you walk me through the structure of the team, including our org charts and reporting structures?

_____

_____

What does success in my role look like? If I am great in this role, what do you think my results will be at the end of the year?

_____

_____

_____

The next questions are around meetings:

When are meetings most often scheduled? (Or, in other words: Is there a norm around when meetings are scheduled? Early? Late? Between 9:00 and 3:00? Over lunch? A mistake first-time managers can make is to violate a norm, like scheduling a meeting at 8:00 a.m. if most folks try to avoid that hour.)

Is there a common duration?

A common format?

Do people usually have pre-reads (summaries or information that is shared in advance of the meeting) and agendas in advance?

These questions are around continuous learning and the logistics of following up with your mentor:

Who do I need to work well with and get to know better? Why?

What do you wish you knew in your first month here that you learned later?

How often should we connect?

How long do you suggest we continue to connect?

Personal Brand

Your personal brand is both how people see you AND how you want others to describe you when you aren't around. You control your brand. As a manager, you control your team's brand as well. Creating a brand, whether personal or for your team, involves consistent behavior, working toward an end goal that others are aware of (and behaving in a way that reflects that end goal), and being the best version of yourself while maintaining authenticity.

SHAPING YOUR BRAND

⊃ Goal: Start to consider how others see you as you begin your new role

When I had four children under the age of eight, things were so busy I worried I'd forget something important, like my computer or my pants. I compressed my work schedule, skipping lunches and arriving early on days I worked from the office. I stacked up meetings in my calendar, sometimes as many as fourteen in a single day. To pull off all these meetings, I would stack my journal, laptop, water bottle, and glasses, and would sometimes racewalk, nearly running, from one meeting to another.

A sponsor of mine was the head of organizational development for our company. One day she asked me, "How do you think people perceive you when you run down the hallway with your gear?" I confidently replied that they would think I was busy and cared about getting my work done. She then said, "What would you think if I told you they thought you looked late and disorganized?"

I was floored. I had never thought people perceived me that way, but it made sense.

She then asked the killer question: "Have you ever seen a man run to a meeting?"

I realized, I never had.

She opened my eyes to the fact that, visually, I was creating a brand for myself, and it was negative and contradicted what I wanted to convey. I immediately slowed down. I walked with purpose. At the beginning of meetings, I would share that I needed to leave at a particular time, so expectations were set for a prompt and timely wrap-up. I started taking deep breaths in between meetings and found a sense of steady calm and purpose with my moves from one meeting to another. Even when my meetings were virtual, I made sure to have a "virtual walk." I would stand, breathe, move a bit, and get my thoughts set for the next meeting. My sponsor's advice had been a game changer for me.

At my next job, her coaching stuck with me. Not only did I carry myself with purpose, I paid close attention to how I built my brand and established a new brand for my team. In the category of "things you don't learn in the interview process," I discovered during my first weeks that my team was ranked statistically dead last in the company.

Over the next eighteen months, I changed everything about how we delivered work assignments, my coaching, quarterly goals, and how we measured progress. When we rose to the top ranking, I would use the phrase "top delivery team in the US" when talking to my partners in technical teams. They would say something went well and I would say, "This is why we are ranked first in the US. We pay attention to testing." Or: "We're the top delivery team because we are especially careful about setting expectations about the timeline." Others started to repeat this phrase around the company: "Hey, see if Christine's team can help. This is a job for the top delivery group." Not only was this the team's brand, but it became mine as well. I was asked to develop training programs at a national level to help other teams mirror what we were doing.

When building your brand, consider the following:

- Which three words do you want people to use when they describe you to others?
- Do you have someone you admire in your company or in another? If so, do you do things they do? For example, I had a leader who confirmed meetings every late afternoon for the following business day. I had another who was very deliberate about giving recognition. I adopted these best practices and started to carry myself like a senior leader, even before it became my title. You can do the same.

The most important thing about your personal brand is to be aware that you have one, and that you can shape it.

Hot tip!

WHY YOU MIGHT FEEL SELF-DOUBT AROUND DAY 60

Madeline texted me near the end of month two, feeling down. She was doing well, so her coworkers acted like she had been there forever. They assumed she knew details about projects and people. The truth? She was still new, and still learning.

Be kind to yourself. Recognize your improvements, but acknowledge that you are still new.

4

Establishing Relationships with Peers

When you meet with peers, you have two goals in mind: form friendships with them and listen for clues and insight that can help you in your new role. While everyone is critical to your success, this group is especially so.

RELATIONSHIPS WITH PEERS

⟳ **Goal: Build lateral strength by forming relationships with peers**

When Madeline started managing a new team, building relationships with her peers felt like extra credit, not the main assignment. Her thinking shifted, however, when she found herself desperate for new hires for her severely understaffed team within just six months. Her team was rebounding from a performance-related departure and morale was very low, so this next hire had to fit.

Layla and Madeline were both looking for someone great to add to their respective teams as soon as possible, so they doubled up and ran interviews together to maximize efficiency. As a side note, Madeline can't recommend this strategy enough, as long as you have built an amicable relationship with your coworker. You can learn a lot from watching your peers interview. Additionally, you'll have the opportunity to receive great feedback from them on your own interview style and approach. They both passed on a few candidates, but after interviewing Davis, they knew he'd be a great fit for the organization and for the roles each was filling. There was only one Davis, of course, so Madeline reached out to Layla to make her case. She explained what her team had experienced over the past few months, including the impact of the team member's departure on her high performers and the continued intensity of her team's workload. She didn't ask for Davis outright, but instead asked for Layla's advice: Was Madeline overemphasizing the importance of fit? Should she focus instead on filling the seat to spread the workload more evenly?

Layla listened and then outlined her own team's situation, which she felt was less dire than Madeline's. She told Madeline, "If I were in your shoes, I would fight to get Davis on my team. Don't underestimate fit," she said, "especially right now. Fit isn't something you can mess around with. My team isn't in recovery, and we can wait a little longer to bring someone in. He's yours!"

The week Davis started, three of Madeline's team members told her he was a great fit for the team and they were glad he had been hired. Their relief was visible in their faces and their voices, which was the goal of bringing him in. Layla's flexibility, and Madeline's positive relationship with her, allowed Madeline to bring in the right person just in time.

In this case, Madeline's peer, Layla, had a positive assessment of her and an orientation toward collaboration. Madeline noted afterward, "To be frank, I've learned my peers will always have an opinion of me. There might be shades of gray, but ultimately, it's binary: they either think I'm doing a good job, or not. Your focus shouldn't necessarily be on what your peers think of you. Instead, you should aim for your peers to have the context of what your team is doing and why."

Most importantly, she notes, "Without Layla's understanding of me, the team's work, and the urgency of my situation, my ask for Davis may have led Layla to assess me, my performance, and my qualities as a teammate differently. Instead, I built my relationship with her by debriefing interviews together, delivering positive feedback on her interview questions, and asking her advice. After establishing this positive relationship, she was more than willing to do me a favor, and it became clear I had earned credibility as a peer leader."

Madeline discovered that when you are a manager, your peers and business partners are important for three reasons: they are important functional relationships to form, they will support you in the months and years ahead, and they are insightful sources of information.

With this group, you have two goals:
1. Form professional friendships
2. Listen for clues about how the organization truly works

To expand on point two, it's a good idea to tune in to clues related to the following questions:
- Who are key teams and people?
- What are top priorities and objectives?
- How are those objectives measured, and how can you help?

We call these clues because many people will give you their opinions. It's only when you consider all these bits of information or "clues" together that you will gain a deeper understanding of the company, its people, and the work. Even if you were an individual contributor in your company before you became a manager, others' perspectives may open your eyes to aspects you hadn't considered.

A communications trainer once noted each time you engage in a conversation, ask a question, or listen with intent, you weave another thread. Ultimately these threads form a fabric. The more thread, the stronger the fabric. Crisis, conflict, and pressure can weigh on the fabric, and the fewer the threads, the more likely the fabric will tear or become damaged. The stronger the fabric, the more the relationship can bear the weight of challenge.

Your first job as a new manager is to focus on starting to form professional friendships and working relationships, especially with your boss, peers, and team. Your second job is to start collecting clues.

By asking key people the same questions during your first month, you can begin to notice trends (perhaps everyone mentions a big change project, or mentions the same person who has answers to tough questions) or you might see divergence (perhaps different people see different top goals, or describe culture differently).

To form friendships and gain valuable insights, try asking questions like these:

Begin with questions to form friendships
- How did you come to work here?
- What do you love about the company?
- What are you proud of from last year?

Next, listen for clues

- What is your top priority/biggest goal for this year?
- What can I do in my role to help you?
- How do you measure progress (key metrics, if they exist)?
- Who are key teams and people I should get to know?

End on a positive note by returning to focus on friendship questions

- Who do you go to when you have a complex question?
- Who do you think I should make a point to meet?

Adapt these questions to suit your own voice and unique circumstances. This is especially important since your target outcomes are to **form friendships and listen for clues.**

Hot tip!

ONE-ON-ONES WITH PEERS

Before you meet with each person, check out their LinkedIn profile. You can jot notes on their conversation page—a person you have in common, how long they've worked at the company, any shared background or interests.

Worksheet: Peers (& Other Key People) Conversations

Name:

Role:

Date:

To form friendships
How did you come to work here?

What do you love about the company?

What are you proudest of from last year?

To listen for clues
What is your top priority or biggest goal for this year?

What can I do in my role to help you?

How do you measure progress (key metrics, if they exist)?

What are key teams I should get to know and understand?

Close with asking about relationships
Who do you go to when you have a complex question?

Who do you think I should make a point to meet?

5

Establishing Relationships with Your Team

As you meet with your team members, focus on getting to know them in two very different ways: as individuals and as a group. Your success hinges on their success. Investing time in understanding your people is worth every moment.

RELATIONSHIPS WITH YOUR TEAM

Goal: Get to know your team in two very different ways: as individuals, and as a group

Your team's success is how your success will be measured. Investing time in building relationships with them is worth every moment.

This next section covers good ways to build relationships with your team. These relationships happen on two levels:

Individually

It's critical to get to know each person individually and figure out how you can most effectively work with them. One-on-one meetings are an excellent way to build trust, learn about work, and start seeing patterns in how a team member completes work, works with others, and works with you.

Collectively

As a collective, your team will have unique dynamics related to how they work together and collaborate (or don't). Keep in mind, these dynamics and patterns were established before you arrived. You may also notice that some of your team members behave differently in a group. Someone who is talkative in one-on-ones may be quiet when they gather with peers. Both dynamics are important to figure out early on.

ONE-ON-ONE MEETINGS WITH TEAM MEMBERS

⟳ **Goal: Establish this functional, lightweight way to know people and manage work**

One-on-one meetings are a great tool for both new and seasoned managers. If you follow the structure of connecting every week with your direct reports, you will naturally get to know them as people and earn their trust. These meetings are an impactful (and simple) way to see how effectively (or not) a person completes work. Here are elements to make meetings highly functional:

Team Member Owns: First, have each team member schedule their one-on-ones with you. Doing this sets a sense of ownership by the team member. Adjust for any conflicts in the scheduling, if the calendaring system allows.

Weekly Cadence: Meetings should be weekly. Keep in mind, these are only partly for you. These meetings give your staff confidence that no matter how busy you get, you will reserve time to give them undivided attention. These meetings should be evergreen, lasting the entire time you are the person's manager. For many managers, the perfect duration is 45 minutes. This gives team members a 15-minute break at the end of the meeting, when nothing is likely to be scheduled. It also gives you a chance to go a bit longer if needed. Experienced managers will likely only need 30 minutes, provided folks arrive on time and the agenda is followed. Find your own best duration, and use your team's time well.

Rapport: Slow down in these meetings. Make sure you are getting to know each person. I asked one of my first bosses what I should ask people the first time I meet them. I had a long list of questions about their work, strategy, and so on. He looked at me and shook his head. "I would consider your first month a success," he said, "if you knew if someone had kids, where they went to school, where they lived, and what they did for fun outside the office." He reminded me that people work hard for someone they like and they want you to know them. An important note here: it takes different people different lengths of time to open up, and some people do not feel comfortable sharing a lot about themselves. It is still on you as a manager to figure out what matters to them outside of work.

Trust: You are building trust during these meetings. If someone shares a concern, listen. Thank them for raising the concern. If someone tells you a potentially embarrassing detail, keep it between yourselves. If you sense they could use advocacy in a tough situation, tell them what you are thinking about doing and ask them if it is okay for you to reach out on their behalf.

Agenda: If you start the one-on-ones with the question, "What do you have for us to go over today?" you set the tone that the person owns the meeting and the agenda. It builds individual accountability expectations for your team member from the beginning.

Early Measurement of Individual Performance: During your first month of meetings, include the questions, "How did last week's work go?" and "What are you working on this week?" Check your notes week over week. Did the person deliver what they planned? Are they organized and planning ahead? Your start as a manager gives you an excuse to ask these questions. It is harder to start this process after you have been working together for a while. Take advantage of being new, and you can ease up from this close management of work as time goes on. These questions will help you learn who you can count on to accurately assess and deliver results. You will also learn who needs more help.

Professional Distance: As a manager, you lose some of your freedom. You can't complain about the company, your peers, or other people on your team with your team. You got this role because you are a steward for the company. Even if you are frustrated with something, you have to keep it to yourself when you are with your team. This may be hard if you were promoted to lead former peers. However, it's critical to practice professionalism, and one-on-ones, though intimate, are not the place for complaints or secrets.

Feedback Culture: When you ask what you can do for a team member, or ask for suggestions on how to be a better manager for them (and ask this consistently), your team members begin to feel comfortable giving feedback about your performance. When you take that in and make adjustments, you build a culture of performance and constant improvement for your team.

Notes and Actions: Close your meetings with a recap of actions. The team member should recap their actions and takeaways, and you should recap yours. Personally, I use an online document to keep a running list of questions for my weekly meeting with my boss. The same document contains notes about action items that require follow-up. Notes and action tracking can be as formal or informal as you want.

Worksheet: Weekly One-on-One Connection with Team Member (First Meeting)

Name:

To build your relationship

How did you come to work here? What do you love about the company? What are you proudest of from last year?

To set the tone for upcoming meetings

This is your meeting, so going forward, I'd like to start with your questions and ways I can help you. What questions do you have for me today?

To gain insight

What should I consider changing and why?

What do you recommend I keep the same and why?

What work do you have planned for this coming week?

How did last week go?

(continued)

(continued)

Close with building relationships

Who do you go to when you have a complex question?

_____

_____

Who do you think I should make a point to meet?

_____

_____

Is there anything I can do for you?

_____

_____

(Close with a positive comment about the conversation—something you will follow up on, or look forward to hearing about.)

Worksheet: Weekly One-on-One Connection with Team Member (Subsequent Meetings)

Use these questions after your first meeting.

Name:

_____

To build your relationship
How was your weekend/morning/lunch/etc.? Start with something personal.

_____

What questions do you have for me today?

_____

To gain insight
Last week, you mentioned you were working on [check previous].
How did things turn out?

_____

_____

What work do you have planned for this coming week?

_____

_____

Do you have any blockers (things that are slowing you down) I could help you with?

_____

_____

Close with building relationships
Is there anything I can do for you?

_____

_____

(Close with a positive comment about the conversation—something you will follow up on, or look forward to hearing about.)

FULL TEAM MEETINGS

⊃ Goal: Create a consistent way to interact together

Inheriting a standing team meeting along with the team was daunting for Madeline, partly because she is generally suspicious of meetings. The recurring meeting had a hyper-defined agenda and was usually used for dispersing information, rather than collaborating or building team connections. When Madeline took the meeting format back to the drawing board, she rebuilt the meeting based on her goals to foster team connections and make the meeting content meaningful.

Figure out the right cadence. For Madeline's group, the right cadence was 30 minutes every other week, in the middle of the week. Folks who were presenting had time to prepare (including Madeline), and the frequency meant it was relatively easy for folks to schedule around it to ensure they could attend.

Open with fun. Even the most buttoned-up team can spare a few minutes for fun. Madeline started each of her team meetings by playing a map-based guessing game for five minutes. At some meetings, the team would guess every location and stack up thousands of points. Some weeks, the team would fail dramatically, leading to laughter from even the quietest team members. Though it was initially met with eye rolls, now the team comes prepared to each meeting with areas of the world they want to guess.

Follow fun with celebration. Once fun wraps, the momentum carries into five minutes of shout-outs. Madeline's team shouts out everything from a nephew's tee ball win to a major migration's successful deployment. Nothing is too small to celebrate, and Madeline writes them all down. Because it happens every meeting, the team comes prepared with successes to share.

Acknowledge peers. At every team meeting, the group votes on the MVP of the past two weeks in a quick poll. If the teammate who receives your vote wins, you are responsible for submitting feedback on why you voted for them (maybe they did you a favor or helped solve a problem). Madeline keeps track of winners, and team members are up for prizes like gifts or an afternoon off once they've been elected MVP a certain number of times. (Note: Keep track of the people nominated. If someone has been overlooked, consider advocating for that person's nomination.)

Keep a rough structure. Madeline's team meetings follow this structure:

- Game (usually a geography guessing game with all involved)
- Shout-outs of recognition (all involved)
- Topic 1 (usually led by one person and involving discussion)
- Topic 2 (same)
- Wrap-up (which will include finding out who will be out of office in the coming days and determining backup plans)

The structure keeps content predictably meaningful and increases attendance and participation.

Ask the team for ideas for the topic sections. When Madeline polled her team, they had great suggestions. People asked for a show-and-tell time for each person to highlight a tool or process they use to stay organized. Some requested peer review of a plan they were working on or sought help to brainstorm solutions. Others asked if Madeline could bring in guest speakers from other teams to discuss project-specific questions. Madeline realized the meetings weren't hers, but the team's. They could and should be part of the agenda-planning process.

Madeline wasn't sure if her meeting format was working, since her team was in the midst of a tough project and energy seemed low. One afternoon she got a call from Leah, a former team member who had transferred departments. Leah shared that she remembered Madeline's team meetings fondly and asked her for guidance on how to set up and run a meeting for her new team.

Standing team meetings can have lasting impact on their participants, especially when carefully constructed and delivered. Keep these ideas in mind:

- Understand your meeting goal. Is it to improve morale? Close a gap and improve how the team works?
- Consider the meeting you have planned and make sure your content serves your main goal.
- Have a loose structure, so people know what to expect.
- Leave holes for different content each week so it isn't boring. (Ideally, you'll eventually crowdsource this part.)

Team meetings are opportunities to get to know how your people work together, consistently share information with everyone, and create a way to collaborate to meet goals. Next up, the focus is on getting to know more about your company.

Learning about the Business

In this section, you are focused on your company. When you understand how the business generates profit, and key areas of focus, you can lead your team in a way that best supports the company.

EARLY UNDERSTANDING OF YOUR COMPANY'S BUSINESS

Goal: Learn about the business and work underway

It's important to make sure you have a complete understanding of the company. If you are switching to a manager role within the same company, you may already grasp some aspects of company operations, but you may not understand specifics. Do a little digging and interviewing to gain a deeper understanding of your organization.

When I started at McDonald's years ago, my first day included a class called "How McDonald's Makes Money." This might surprise you: McDonald's revenue structure is not oriented around fast food sales. In some countries, McDonald's owns the land all the restaurants are built on, which makes McDonald's similar to a real estate investment trust (REIT). The profits come from "rent" charged on the property, based on sales. In other countries, McDonald's can't own property, so a licensing fee is charged. Certain McDonald's restaurants can generate more "rent" revenue than entire countries. Some restaurants are owned directly by the company, and others are owned by franchisees, with McDonald's providing (and charging for) services. When I understood that revenue comes from property, services, and (disproportionately) different geographic markets, this knowledge helped me better understand the impact of my teams' projects and guided my decision-making.

The following worksheet can be filled in at once after a conversation with your boss, or over time, as you have conversations with others. Your familiarity with these key areas is critical to both your understanding of the work and priorities, and more importantly, to you being able to communicate them to your team.

You'll want to explore the following areas:
- Your company and its business model
- How your team's work fits into the company's big picture goals, and how the goals will be measured
- Basic finances

Hot tip!

WHEN YOU SEEK INSIGHT ABOUT THE BUSINESS

Before you start asking questions, conduct online searches. Read the 10-K report (this can be found online if your company is public) and/or the company website.

Remember: Before you start researching and asking questions about the business, read the 10-K, company website statements about strategy, and online articles. Get external insight before you ask folks questions internally. Your research will help you look prepared and make your conversations more effective. Note, this exploration can be done even before you start your position.

Worksheet: Understanding the Business

To understand the business, talk with leaders, starting with your boss, to build your understanding

How do we make money?

Does our profit come from multiple sources? If so, what is the split of the sources?

How do we tie compensation to performance? If there is a bonus structure, what does that look like for all team members? How are we tracking our goals and targets? (This question is critical. A company might say, "We want to diversify," but if there are no compensation goals tied to adding new clients, diversification likely won't happen. Essentially, these questions examine the tie between stated strategy and team rewards.)

What were our results last year, and what are our targets this year?

Are there changes we are trying to make as an organization to hit those targets?

Is there a published strategy I can learn about and tie my team's strategy to?

How do we communicate company progress against our goals?

CHECK-IN ⟳ Strong Start

Are you tired? Good! This is hard work. When you layer learning names, finding your way around, and figuring out human dynamics on top of building relationships and looking for clues (that is, learning about the job, team, and company), it's a LOT.

Take a breath. You've made it this far. Let's check in.
Go down the list and summarize what you've accomplished.

- ○ Established a professional relationship with your boss
- ○ Set one-on-one cadence with your boss
- ○ Generally figured out access to systems, finding your way around the office or virtual landscape
- ○ Met with these peers/key people:

_____   _____

_____   _____

_____   _____

_____   _____

- ○ Scheduled and structured group team meeting
- ○ Learned key foundational information about the business, and most importantly, how your team fits into the picture
- ○ Established one-on-one cadence with each team member:

_____   _____

_____   _____

_____   _____

- ○ Developed a sense of how you want to appear and how to define your personal brand
- ○ Scheduled interaction with your sponsor/mentor

Congratulations! Starting strong takes a lot of energy, focus, and structure. A productive, tough set of learning objectives is behind you. You have a strong foundation to build on.

Early Learning:

Team's Work in Flight, Initial Manager Objectives, Lightweight Team Objectives

This section will focus on the difference between goals and objectives, learning about the work your team has underway, and setting initial personal objectives. You are starting to form your plan to lead their delivery.

WORK, GOALS, AND OBJECTIVES

⟳ **Goal: Learn about the work, goals, objectives, and measurements for your team**

Once you have a sense of the company's goals and how profits are driven, it's a good next step to focus on work and priorities for your team and yourself.

It's critical to understand that work and progress are usually measured in two different ways:

- **Goals.** These are usually set on an annual basis. They may be noted in company presentations or in HR systems that track employees. Some companies have specific goals for each team, while others only have top-level company targets.
- **Objectives.** Unlike goals, which are high-level and long-term, objectives can usually be completed and measured in 90 days or less. They typically support top goals, but can also be focused on short-term improvements for individuals or teams.

The next worksheet focuses on your team's in-progress work, how it will be measured, and team member roles in the work. While your boss is likely to be the best person to ask, you can also learn by asking and observing your team. It's worth finding quiet time to read recent status reports and familiarize yourself with current work and goals.

My daughter's second-grade soccer team hadn't won a game all year. Her team was part of a recreation league emphasizing learning, so each girl had the opportunity to play every position during the season. This gave everyone a chance to understand the different roles on the field. Most coaches relied on a random rotation, telling the girls where to go at the start of each half. Teams usually picked their own names, and this one had called themselves the Cheetos (orange shirts).

In the second-to-last game of the year, the Cheetos went into half-time tied. You could see hope on everyone's faces for a first-time win. Knowing there was a chance, the coach focused on the girls in the striker positions with the most scoring opportunities. She talked to the strikers about passing, taking chances, and running to the ball instead of waiting for it. When she moved to the other players, the referee whistled to start the second half. The coach didn't have a chance to talk over a game plan with the other members of the team. As the girls ran onto the field, one yelled back to the coach, "We figured it out! We are leaving Emma in goal because she loves it there, and Sadie wanted to play center defender because she is fast. Beth wanted to rest, so I am staying in for her."

The girls had figured out a strategy without her guidance. The team won their first game and celebrated with ice cream. The coach noted that there were four strategies going on in that second half (scoring, goal-tending, substitutions, and defense), and she had only set up one of them. The others came from the team.

Business is the same. A good manager gives the team the target, provides space for them to do it their way, and celebrates when results are achieved.

These next sections cover learning about the team's current work that you need to achieve together and setting your own initial objectives related to that work. Assigning lightweight objectives to everyone your team for the quarter creates an opportunity for you to observe and learn more about them. As they make progress, take note of their insights and how they approach work.

Worksheet: Understanding the Team's Work in Flight

As a new manager, you have inherited a team, their existing culture, any work that is in flight, and target objectives that were set beforehand. Learning about the work in flight, and how you can support it, is critical to your success. This worksheet focuses on questions to discuss with your boss around the team's work that is underway.

To understand the team's work

What work is in flight for my team right now?

Where can I look to learn more about it (status reports, tracking systems)?

What is each person on the team working on now? (If your team is large or you have multiple teams reporting to you, you should have the org chart handy as a reference to names and titles.)

Have I inherited specific annual goals for the team? If so, what is our progress against them for this year?

What should we be focusing on most of all?

Do we already have objectives in place (short-term targets to achieve or improve in the next 90 days or so)?

If not, do you have objectives in mind for the team and me for the next 90 days?

Are there any issues with the work that I need to be aware of? Do any issues need to be addressed immediately?

MANAGER'S FIRST OBJECTIVES

⟳ **Goal: Don't overthink, but do come up with a first list of targets for yourself**

Once you have learned about what the team has underway, create a summary of your own personal objectives. Ideally, objectives are created and measured quarterly (January 1 through March 31, April 1 through June 30, and so on).

For your first set of personal objectives, use whatever time is left in the quarter to achieve what you can. For example, if you start on July 15, come up with a list of objectives to accomplish before September 30. If you start on September 20, it would be difficult to plan and execute objectives before September 30, so it's best to think about the next quarter and set your objectives through the end of December.

Your first set of objectives will likely revolve around four areas: onboarding activities, onboarding goals, work to deliver with the team, and a top goal for yourself as the team manager.

For onboarding, you'll consider activities first: Which onboarding activities do I need to complete to start strong? What training do I need to complete? Which key peers should I meet? Make sure your activities have target dates and that you have a good sense of why each matters.

Next, as you consider your first quarter or your onboarding period, what is most important to do first? Do you need to establish a relationship with the Business Relationship Manager on another team so you can plan for a big project next year? Is there a team problem to solve? Does your boss want you to build a deep understanding of the business? There should be one strategic focus for your onboarding, in addition to the flurry of administration of onboarding tasks.

Next, as you look at the top three to five deliverables or objectives for your team, you will identify your specific role to help. Do you need to intervene and make a change? Do you need to use your subject expertise to help solve a problem? Do you need to take a position of observation and only engage when needed? Identify your individual role specifically to help their work underway.

Last, confirm you have a clear understanding of what your boss believes success looks like for your first year, and add an objective to your list to confirm you are doing something now to move toward this goal.

Worksheet: Manager's First Objectives

Onboarding activities

ONBOARDING ACTIVITY	NOTES	TARGET DATE	DATE COMPLETED
e.g., Compliance training	Diversity, Ethics, Guidelines for Stock program	Within 30 days / July 31	July 20
e.g., Peer Meeting: Laura	Runs Finance. Learn about headcount budgets	August 15	

Overall initial onboarding objective

Confirm your boss's expectation of what your onboarding period outcome should be, and confirm you have objectives to help meet this expectation.

Ask your boss:
If this is a very successful first few months, what have I accomplished for you?
Add your notes of any specific objectives to achieve the above.

Manager's role in team work objectives for the next ~90 days

Confirm the top three to five priorities/objectives and key results for the team as a whole, and your role:

RANKING	TEAM OBJECTIVE	MY ROLE	TARGET DATE
e.g. 1	*Complete the compliance audit by the 31st.*	*Watch the physical audit in particular; the process audit usually goes well and will only need my help if they ask.*	*3/30*
e.g. 2	*Sell 1400 units.*	*Set targets for each person. Shadow sales calls.*	*3/26*
1.			
2.			
3.			

Getting started on a great first year

Lastly, ask about what the first-year goal looks like, and check to make sure you have created an objective for yourself for the next 90 days that advances you toward that goal as well.

Ask your boss:
If a year from now everyone says I have done a great job, what have I accomplished?
Add your notes of any specific objectives to start on now to achieve the above.

Worksheet: Initial Lightweight Team Member Objectives

If it feels hard to set quarterly objectives for yourself when you are brand-new, it is nearly impossible to do the same thing for your team members (unless your company already did so). Instead of setting deep or detailed objectives, consider doing something lightweight at first. As you hold one-on-one meetings with your team members during your first weeks, talk with them about their development, work or project commitments, and build out the following list:

TEAM MEMBER	CURRENT FOCUS/COMMITMENT HOW CAN YOU, AS THEIR MANAGER, ASSIST?	DATE DUE
e.g., Iris	*Completing web development class. Assistance: It would be great if we could find a web developer for Iris to talk to when she has questions after her class completes.*	*6/20*
e.g., Pat	*Taking over the consumer experience product road map. Assistance: We will meet in a few weeks so Pat can present the initial summary, and we can talk about the plan to complete.*	*5/15*

CHECK-IN ⮌ Initial Assessment of Work, Initial Objectives for Yourself and Your Team

The center of what you will do is lead and help your team deliver work. Check in, and note what you have accomplished.

○ What are the top three to five things the team is working on, and how will you measure success?

Work in Flight   *Measurement*

_____   _____

_____   _____

_____   _____

_____   _____

_____   _____

_____   _____

○ To build on the above—are you confident your boss would agree that you have the right priority?

○ Have you built out objectives for yourself for this first quarter in your new role that support completion of your onboarding, support the team's work for the next 90 days, and provide a sense of how you will start on your goal of having a great first year?

○ Picture a peer stopping you in the hallway and asking, "How is the new role going? What is the biggest thing you need to get done?" How would you answer?

○ If the CEO asks what your team is working on, how would you answer so you tie your team's work to big-picture business goals?

○ This is not essential, but do you have a sense of each individual team member's commitments for the upcoming weeks, in terms of their own personal delivery? (Not essential, but useful to know.)

Congratulations! Now that you understand the work and what is expected of you in these first months, you can lean in to help the team deliver.

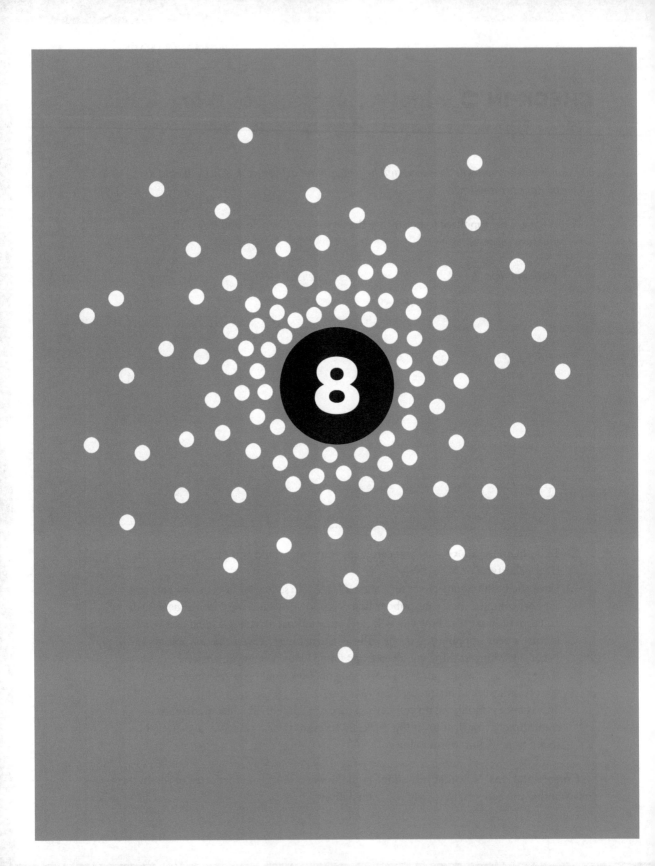

The Heart of Management:

Goals and Objectives

This section is best used when you know more about your team and are ready to add some detail to how you are managing work and people. Your first objectives were lightweight and focused on your first few months. This section helps you consider goals and objectives fully for those quarters that follow your first.

MANAGING WORK

⟳ **Goal: Translate strategy to work objectives every 90 days**

When I joined Dell, each manager was expected to have quarterly objectives for each of their people. It seemed like a lot of work, but I learned to love the process.

If you have worked at a company that only sets yearly goals for staff, I bet you have seen:

- Procrastinators who put off working on their goals until November
- Goals that were set at the start of the year that became irrelevant by the end of the year
- Lofty goals that were unrealistic or vague (e.g., "Build the team's brand") where your supposed goal achievement or failure was dependent on your boss's subjective assessment

Dell showed me a new way to look at individual goals. Instead of planning yearly goals, we planned objectives for 90-day periods. We set no more than three, so the manager and team members could focus. At the end of the year, we had twelve results (three objectives from each quarter) and a depth of insight about each person's results.

I learned:

Anyone can change anything in 90 days. Do you have a team member who needs to improve email or messaging clarity? They can practice and make improvements within 90 days. Do you have a quality problem in your development team? Focus on bugs for 90 days, and you will see the quality rise.

90 days is a great duration. It's long enough to achieve something, but short enough to complete the experiment of making the change and measuring the outcome. In the next quarter, you can potentially move on to something else. Markets change, customer needs change, humans grow and develop.

You don't have to be perfect; this is a chance to learn. When you are setting goals for a year, you need to have mythical capabilities to come up with ideas that are measurable, realistic, and relevant. On the other hand, the process of creating only a few objectives each quarter gives you a chance to grow as a leader. Maybe an idea you had for an objective didn't work out well. Good news! You get to do something new soon.

The following worksheets provide guidance on how to set 90-day objectives, first for your team and then for individual team members.

Worksheet: Setting Objectives for the Team as a Whole

Remind yourself of the company's strategic goals and key measurements that will be used to measure success. Is the company mainly concerned about year-over-year growth? Expansion of a particular market? Customer acquisition? Increase in profitability?

Summarize the top one to three key company goals here:

STRATEGY	HOW SUCCESS WILL BE MEASURED

Now, think about your team. What work is your team doing to support these strategic targets? Perhaps your team is responsible for sales in one of the emerging markets, or for developing a new application that will release midyear and will drive app downloads and revenue. Challenge yourself: Make sure you have an objective (a business goal) AND that you know how you will measure your success, or recognize that you miss the mark (your key results). Putting the goal and quantitative measurement together, and identifying how they tie to company strategy, is a powerful approach to planning.

OBJECTIVE (Team's business goal)	KEY RESULT (Measurement used to check progress)	LIST OF POSSIBLE WORK (To contribute to achieving key results)	WHICH PART OF THE COMPANY STRATEGY DOES THIS SUPPORT?

Next, ask yourself: Are there important things your team does that might not directly contribute to strategy but are critical to the company's operations? Perhaps you support the research group, or provide disaster recovery services, or do the monthly financial closes. Note those as well. Some teams have no operational work, and others do. If your team does, note those below.

MAIN OPERATIONAL WORK	KEY RESULT (MEASUREMENT USED TO CHECK PROGRESS, IF POSSIBLE)

Now, think about your role in all of this. Taking the objectives and results from above, confirm your own contributions to these key work efforts.

PRIORITY RANKING	TEAM OBJECTIVE	MY ROLE
1		
2		
3		

SETTING OBJECTIVES FOR EACH TEAM MEMBER

⟳ **Goal: Take the next steps to understand each person's objectives to support the team objective**

Now that you have a clear understanding of the team's objectives, take the next steps to consider team members separately so everyone on the team has a personal way to contribute to results.

A week or so before the new quarter starts, sit down with each team member. Make sure you have one to three objectives and key expected results for each person. The objectives and target results should be different for everyone. If your sales team has a quarterly objective of $5 million, your senior enterprise sales person may have a personal goal of $2 million, and each junior sales person may have goals of $500,000 each. Your marketing person might have an objective to increase marketing impressions by 12 percent.

Everyone uniquely supports the business target.

Each person should have a developmental objective, too. Ideally, this objective would come from the employee themself, though you can collaborate on setting it together. Newer team members might need help coming up with developmental objectives, but you can and should expect your more senior people to bring you their own ideas for areas of growth. Encourage your team members to identify an area that, once improved, could bolster their career and reputation. Perhaps a project manager would like to work on her presence while presenting. Another may need to bring more data points into status reporting. A new graduate may need to complete training and certification.

Before the next quarter starts, ask yourself:
- Does each person have at least one or two business objectives?
- Do their business objectives have realistic measurements that are within their control to achieve?
- Does each person have a developmental objective?
- Does that developmental objective have an expected outcome?

When you engage in this type of planning at the beginning of the quarter, you and your team start out with a shared expectation of what performance looks like. It doesn't matter whether a team member works in-office, remotely, hybrid, or on the road. Each of you knows what success is and how it will be measured.

This work of helping people frequently set their work targets and understand how their work supports the goals of the business is the heart of being a manager.

Worksheet: Individual Objectives

Name:

WORK OBJECTIVE (Goal to accomplish in next 90 days)	MEASUREMENT (How we will measure success)	WORK AND DEADLINES TO SUPPORT THE OBJECTIVE

DEVELOPMENTAL OBJECTIVE (Personal development in next 90 days)	MEASUREMENT (How this supports career growth)	ACTIVITIES AND TIMELINES

Rhythm, Results & Strengths

This section focuses on settling into a rhythm and achieving initial results. Keep in mind, these tasks are difficult to do without first gathering insights about your people and the work you are doing together. I strongly suggest collecting that information first.

GETTING INTO A RHYTHM

⤳ **Goals: Settle into a rhythm, focus on initial results, and learn about team strengths**

After you have critical mechanics down—you are in systems and meetings, you have connected to peers and sponsors who support your success, and you have an initial understanding of work—you can go a level deeper in two ways:

1. Gain a better understanding of your team's work and how to measure results
2. Gain a better understanding of your team's strengths

The next sections guide you through both processes.

Hot tip!

BENEFITS OF TEAM MEETINGS FOR RHYTHM

If you haven't already established team meetings, or you think you don't need them, consider this:

One of my favorite leaders would hold a department huddle every Tuesday at 9 a.m. Team members were expected to convene in a wide hallway in the building, where the leader would share anything he had learned from leadership meetings and business partners to help us better understand the business. He would relay insights such as:

- *Results rose in a particular sector; we should expect to see more projects there.*
- *The new CXO is starting in a few weeks and has indicated she will increase focus on data analytics.*
- *It is [NAME'S] anniversary/birthday/return from paternity leave!*
- *Each week, the team would transfer the care of a plant he named Pat. Pat the Plant went to someone who had gone above and beyond for the week. If Person X received the plant the week before, they were expected to bring the plant back (alive!) the following week and announce who they named as "above and beyond" for that week. And the pattern continued each week, creating awareness of members' contributions and progress.*
- *After the leader shared any relevant news or insights, and Pat the Plant was passed along, we had the opportunity to ask him any question we wanted.*

The meeting lasted 15 minutes and was a low-effort way to stay in tune with the company, feel connected to our leader, and laugh together.

If your team doesn't have a department or team huddle or weekly meeting, consider adding one to build a sense of continuity and share key insights.

RHYTHM OF INDIVIDUAL WEEKLY RESULTS

⟳ Use one-on-one meetings both to build relationships and as a tool
to start measuring results

As you create and establish work patterns, it's a good idea to return to your prior evaluations to gain insights. First, go to your team one-on-one notes from the past two weeks.

Ask yourself:
- Did this person complete what they said they would two weeks ago?
- Did this person complete what they said they would the week after that?
- Did they share information clearly?
- How would I classify them, out of the following categories?
    - Strong: needing minimal oversight
    - Developing: needing situational oversight
    - Early stages: needing structured support

Write a note to yourself about each person and let this simple assessment guide how you adapt your one-on-one meetings going forward.

Give each employee what they personally need by repeating this process of looking back at their last two one-on-ones.

Summarize this information in the worksheet on the next page.

**Worksheet: Quick Check:
One-on-One Results and Need for Support**

As you plan to support your team members, you will support each in different ways that are reflective of what they need.

- **For a strong person,** your strategy for support might be focused on making sure they get exposure to leadership, a challenging new assignment, or an opportunity to coach others.
- **For someone who is developing,** you may find them a subject-matter expert to shadow or work closely with. You may give them a developmental assignment in which they work on a project in stages, under your supervision.
- **For someone who is struggling,** you may try to remove distractions from their day so they can focus more closely on work. You may seek appropriate training courses to help them improve skills, or add regular touchpoints with them to provide more feedback and support.

Recognize that each person will need something different, and you will build trust when you can explain the individual and appropriate support you are giving them.

NAME	THIS PAST WEEK COMPLETE? Y/N	TWO WEEKS AGO COMPLETE? Y/N	STRONG, DEVELOPING, OR EARLY?	MY PLAN TO SUPPORT

RHYTHM OF EARLY OBJECTIVE AND KEY RESULTS FOR THE QUARTER

➲ **Slow down, and consider how your team is doing on the original early understanding of goals you identified**

Next, go to your notes on gaining an early understanding of the team's work and setting your own initial objectives.

Consider these:

- Has my team made measurable progress toward our objectives? (If not, figure out what to focus on during the next weeks to help.)
- Have I received any signals from leadership that we are doing well or doing poorly?
- Does our method of measuring progress make sense? Or do I have other ideas?
- Does it make sense to change certain objectives (targets in the next three months) or goals (targets for the business year)? If so, which ones?

DISCERNING TEAM MEMBER STRENGTHS

⊃ Goal: Get the best from your team by understanding and leveraging individuals' strengths

Now that you have been working with your team for a while and are in a rhythm, you are likely getting insight into each person's capabilities.

Much research has been done on uncovering team members' strengths. Do you know the objectively worst way to find out what someone is good at? Ask them what they are good at. Seriously.

It's better to ask:

What makes you happy? Another way to ask is, "If you came into work today and enjoyed every moment, what did that day look like?" Or, "What are you most proud of?"

Researchers have found that when people are happy at work, it is usually because they complete work at an "excellent level." This means:

- People compliment them.
- They get things done quickly and with few errors.
- The results are clear to the person and others.
- They feel valued.

Treating everyone equally through work assignments (for example, giving each person the same project portfolio blend, or splitting analytic and interactive work equally) can have you missing the chance to get the best out of your team. Different people thrive with different types of work. Start building your understanding of team members to increase success.

When meeting with your team members and asking the questions above, look for nonverbal signals. When someone talks about work they enjoy:

- Their eyes light up
- They have increased gesticulation/hand movements
- They lean forward
- They smile

When you see these signs, the team member is talking about their strengths.

Many managers supplement their observations with tools like Insights Discovery or Gallup StrengthsFinder to help team members gain a better understanding of themselves and fellow team members. This could be something you pursue, both for the insight it brings and as a shared activity to pull your team together.

Reviewing team members' strengths and alignment to work should become a yearly practice. As each of us grows and improves, we start to develop new strengths. Your team members' emerging strengths will create opportunities for you and the team to solve new problems for your company.

The next worksheet includes questions you can ask your team members to help uncover strengths in a conversational format. Beneath each question is a brief explanation of its purpose.

What makes you happy? Which parts of work do you enjoy most?
Answers here should point you in the right direction. When you ask the questions
below, those answers will add layers and clarity.

What are you proudest of from your last year's work?
Pride can show authentic, personal reflection on achievement.

If you came into the work day, enjoyed every minute of it, and
wrapped up saying, "This was a GREAT day," what happened?
To add insight, you can ask, "What did you work on?" or, "Did you work alone or with others?"
Ask clarifying questions so you can get to the core of what they enjoyed.

What compliments do you usually receive from people around the office?
Or, what do people usually seek you out for?
Here you are looking for external validation of the person's assessment.

It's important to note that if you feel you have trust built with the person, you can ask them which parts of their job they are most likely to procrastinate on or wish were different. If you haven't built trust, this question won't work as well.

Take notes, listen carefully.

Celebrate strengths with your team.

Worksheet: Discerning Team Member Strengths

Take notes. Listen carefully. Celebrate strengths with your team members.

Ask your team member
What makes you happy? Which parts of work do you enjoy most?

_____

_____

What are you proudest of from the last year here?

_____

_____

**If you came into the work day, enjoyed every minute of it,
and wrapped up saying, "This was a GREAT day," what happened?**
Follow-up questions, if you need them: What did you work on?
Did you work alone? With others?

_____

_____

What do people compliment you on the most here, or seek you out for?

_____

_____

ONLY if you feel you have built trust with the person, ask them:
**Which parts of your job are you most likely to procrastinate on or wish
were different?**

_____

_____

Hot tip!

PUTTING PEOPLE WHERE THEY THRIVE

When you understand the setting in which a team member thrives, you can put them in it more often. This is especially impactful if it is a setting you don't thrive in yourself and their skills complement yours.

When thinking about whether someone thrives in a particular area, consider the following questions:

- *Is this person thorough?*
- *Are they fast at completing certain work?*
- *Do they have good radar for assessing a situation?*
- *Are they organized?*
- *Are they diligent?*
- *Are they courageous—willing to take on challenging work or raise hard questions?*
- *Are they strategic?*
- *Do they have specific areas of expertise?*
- *Do they thrive in groups or in solitary pursuits?*
- *Are they well-loved? Respected? Feared?*
- *Are they comfortable in chaos?*
- *Are they comfortable in operational excellence (keeping things steady and running)?*

TEAM WORKLOAD AND BALANCE

⊃ Goal: Try the Goldilocks Exercise

A key part of rhythm is determining when your team's workload is out of balance.

When you are able, start a quarterly (or monthly, if needed) process where you check in on your team. My check-in exercise is modeled after the children's story, Goldilocks and the Three Bears. In the story, a little girl stumbles upon a cottage in the woods. The owners (a family of bears) are out for the day, so she investigates the house. Each time she finds something new, like chairs to sit on, she discovers that one is usually too hard, another too soft, and one is just right.

In the "Goldilocks" exercise I use with my teams, I sit down with an individual and ask:

- **Are you too busy?**
- **Not busy enough?**
- **Or just right?**

It's a great kickoff question. It's simple, unambiguous, and sets the tone to start to talk about work.

Asking these questions each quarter builds trust. You set the expectation that work evolves. It's okay for someone to have too much or too little. Once you realize that, you can make adjustments as a team. You build empathy and trust as a manager, and also drive engagement. An overworked person loses heart; a bored person loses interest. While this exercise is about balancing work, it is equally about caring for your team.

Worksheet: Goldilocks (Workload)

TEAM MEMBER	TOO MUCH	TOO LITTLE	JUST RIGHT	NOTES	ANY ACTION TO TAKE? *(Shift work? Change assignments?)*

CHECK-IN ➲ Rhythm, Results, Strengths

You are likely getting into a rhythm, getting work done, asking harder questions, and seeing the path forward.

You are likely also tired because the well-defined support systems you used when you first started (like your onboarding programs) are no longer part of your day.

Take a breath. You've made it this far. Let's check in.

Go down the list and summarize what you've accomplished.

- ◯ You evaluated your team, and you have a good sense of who is strong, developing, or in early stages.
- ◯ You have a plan to support each person.
- ◯ You have an initial sense of what your personal objectives are and how you are doing.
- ◯ You have a sense of the team's objectives.
- ◯ You have a sense of yearly goals.
- ◯ You have a sense of how the team is currently doing against those objectives and goals.
- ◯ You have thought about whether immediate changes are needed and have a plan to make adjustments as needed.
- ◯ You better understand your team, and you have a sense of each person's strengths:

Person   Strength

_____   _____

_____   _____

_____   _____

- ◯ You use the Goldilocks system to assess workload.
- ◯ You understand who needs more/less work.
- ◯ You have taken action to adjust work accordingly.

You continue to build key relationships:
- ◯ You have consistent weekly one-on-ones with your boss, where you bring notes and questions.
- ◯ You have consistent one-on-ones with your team members.
- ◯ You have meetings with key peers.

Congratulations! A productive set of work is behind you. You have continued to build your strong foundation.

10

Coaching

While you were once a successful individual contributor, you are now counted on to lift the performance of others. Another challenge of leadership is getting the best from your team. This section focuses on how to build their success. And ultimately your own.

IN-THE-MOMENT COACHING WHEN THINGS GO WRONG

⮑ **Goal: Help your folks make specific adjustments in context**

I vividly remember an instance when I received coaching in the moment.

I was in a meeting with my peers. I was frustrated when they were arguing about how to report the completion percentage of a very complex project. They were behind and suggested we change the measurement of complete (though we were only partially done) to include progress on planning. This would have pushed the completion percentage up without an actual increase in completed milestones.

I pushed back and said, "This is disingenuous and misleads our leadership." Immediately, one of my peers responded, "Are you calling me a liar and challenging my honesty?" His in-the-moment observation helped me realize I had used my words carelessly. I apologized immediately. I said, "You're right. I said that poorly and I owe you an apology."

His feedback in the moment helped me notice something. I could feel myself getting anxious and frustrated. I should have taken a breath and realized he was anxious too. I should have found more diplomatic ways to express my thoughts. I was able to apologize and recover. I did hold firm on reporting accuracy and was able to preserve our relationship.

It's rare to give feedback like that in front of a group. I don't recommend it, unless, like the two of us, you have developed deep trust with the other person.

If you were my boss and had observed this firsthand, you could have stepped into the conversation and reframed what I had said in order to help de-escalate. Then, when the meeting was over, you could have pulled me aside for a quick conversation. By asking smart follow-up questions, you could catch me while I am still feeling the stress of the moment. Try asking, "Hey, how do you think that meeting went?" Then, follow up with questions about how I was feeling, how he reacted, and what I could have done differently. At this point, details will still be fresh in my mind (how I felt, what specifically was said), which makes the situation easier to recognize and diagnose. Three months later, I might not even remember this meeting. In the moment, I can think about what I might have done differently.

The moment matters.

Hot tip!

IN-THE-MOMENT COACHING VS. PERFORMANCE REVIEWS

Performance reviews come annually, or sometimes biannually. But don't think you have to wait for a review to help someone on your team make an adjustment. Addressing an issue IN THE MOMENT (or shortly after) is often more impactful than saving an issue for a review meeting. Addressing positive behavior in the moment is equally critical. Your compliments and observations immediately reinforce good actions and give your team member a chance to do more right away.

Worksheet: Negative Feedback, In the Moment

This checklist is for behavior you observe only. (Don't give feedback in this way if you heard about something secondhand, more about this on the next page.)

○ **Keep it casual and conversational.** Don't add stress or formality by scheduling a meeting called "Feedback." It will create anxiety with your team member (and you).

○ **Now or soon.** Don't wait too long. (The only exception here is if you are too mad; then, by all means, try to fit in a five-minute meditation first.)

○ **Have them start the conversation.** Ask them how they think a meeting/interaction went. Listen closely. Use questions like, "Why do you think . . .?" and, "How did you feel . . .?" Most bad moments have aspects of emotion. Try to have them express how they felt in the moment.

○ **Ask questions.** If you feel there was something the person missed, ask about it. "Why do you think Will got angry?" and, "Why do you think the team wasn't ready?"

○ **Frame any suggestions in the positive for their career.** Say something like: "As a future senior engineer, this is going to be a critical part of your role—managing through tough architectural meetings. I think if you can figure out how to involve others/share feedback more directly/share feedback less directly, it will make you even more effective."

○ **Ask what they might do differently next time.**

○ **Suggest follow-ups** like an apology, a check-in with someone, or another next step.

○ **Say thank you** for talking (these conversations are hard) and **end with a smile.**

You are in this conversation together because you believe in them.

Worksheet: Negative Feedback, Delayed

The first checklist is for behavior you observe only. Sometimes behavior is escalated to you. You don't see it, but you hear about it. This page focuses on secondhand feedback.

The cardinal rule is that your reply should be (assuming this is true), **"Gosh that doesn't sound like Beth."** If you reply immediately with, "This is unacceptable, I will go yell at Beth now," you reinforce that you aren't surprised by Beth's supposed actions, and you do her a disservice. What if the complainer was confused? Or, what if Beth did exactly what you had asked her to do, and the complainer didn't like it?

The second cardinal rule is to ask, **"What did Beth say when you talked to her?"** Model behavior and encourage others to be honest and solve issues together. Suggest that the person pursue follow-up directly, and ask Beth to be collaborative.

If this is something you should get involved in, start a conversation with Beth to get her perspective of the story.

○ Talk to Beth. Relay that someone mentioned a meeting/interaction that didn't go well, but didn't share many details, and you wanted to check in. How is she?

○ Ask her to give you an explanation.

○ Ask curious questions.

○ If you can tell from her explanation that she made a mistake, ask her how she was feeling in the moment. Ask if she felt her behavior helped or hurt the situation? If she could redo the situation, would she have done anything differently? Then, suggest appropriate follow-up.

○ If you discover Beth was in the right, go back to the person who first approached you, and suggest they talk to each other again. Share your perspective about why you support Beth's approach.

How you handle this sets the tone for collaboration and trust. You are in this conversation together because you believe in them.

IN-THE-MOMENT COACHING
WHEN THINGS GO WELL

⊃ **Goal: Reinforce valuable behavior in your folks**

Positive feedback can also be effective in the moment. Whenever I see good behavior, especially for a person on my team, I make sure to send a note or comment:

"Nice job noticing that the Cosmo squad was late with their work. I appreciated how you used the morning development Agile stand meeting to show that the work had been blocked. I also like how you pulled Marley aside afterwards to talk about options."

"Great question today about pursuing alternative options. I appreciate that you spoke up during the meeting instead of waiting until afterwards. Since the key decision-makers were in the room, you made great use of their time and got an answer quickly."

"I appreciate that you complimented Mateo on how he escalated and solved that bug. He doesn't always get credit for his work, and I know he hopes to be promoted. You helped both Mateo and the team by sharing his approach."

Everyone responds to positive feedback. You will notice three things about this feedback:

1. It was in the moment (or close).
2. It was specific and included behaviors I want to reinforce, in the hopes they happen more often.
3. Where I could, I talked about the impact of the action so the team member can understand the impact on the larger organization.

Worksheet: Weekly Positive Feedback to Team

Years ago, when I worked at Dell, a senior vice president would call employees on Friday afternoons to give them positive feedback. He asked his direct reports who on their teams was making a difference, and then he reached out to say thank you. After a particularly hard week, he called me as I was driving home and complimented me on how I had solved a problem. I was so thrilled that such a senior person knew my work. I grinned all the way home and came back the next week with renewed energy.

Because of the power of positive feedback, I've made it a priority to give each person on my team positive feedback each week.

Set a goal for yourself to find something good to say about each person this week:

PERSON	COMPLIMENT	COMPLETE? Y/N

PERSON	COMPLIMENT	COMPLETE? Y/N

NOT EVERYONE WANTS CAREER GROWTH

⟳ **Goal: Understand who does and doesn't want career progression, and adjust**

The title of this section sounds negative, but the truth is, not everyone is in growth mode. And that can be great for your team.

I once worked with a quiet man in the finance department. He wore cardigan sweaters, came in smiling each morning around 9:30, took long lunches, and left early each day. He was in a fairly junior role in the team but had graying hair. One day, as he was helping me with a project, I mentioned that he could grow far beyond his current role.

He burst out laughing. It turns out, he used to be the chief financial officer (CFO) of one of our other divisions. After his mother was diagnosed with dementia, he planned to retire early to spend time with her. He mentioned to one of his peers that he worried about getting bored, so they came up with a plan. He accepted a junior role at the division near his mother's care facility. He was able to do the work of a junior person in a fraction of the time of his colleagues. He also stepped in to support the new CFO of this division as a mentor.

In return, he was able to drive to his mother's facility each morning and play music for her while they had breakfast together. He'd return for lunch and take her on walks; then, he would come back in the afternoon, when they would work on puzzles or read together.

He didn't want to grow his career, but he was a contributing member of the team.

This opened my eyes. I started making sure I understood what each of my team members wanted. Was career progression a goal? Or were they interested in staying in their current role?

I was surprised when I discovered who wanted to stay in their current spot:

- *A technical operations person who loved the daily, consistent support he gave to others*
- *A brilliant engineer who never wanted to manage people; she only wanted to work on interesting technical problems*
- *A young parent who didn't want to miss a moment with his kids and realized the next step in his career would necessitate travel*

There can be a bias that each of us needs to seek constant growth, but sometimes we put nonwork areas ahead. When the manager is on the same page as the employee, this is powerful for both parties. The manager doesn't push for a growth plan the person doesn't want, and they both have a shared expectation that, in exchange for a manageable workload and even-keel work life, the person will likely forgo major compensation increases and promotions. The manager then gets a responsible, reliable person, and the person gets what they need out of their professional life.

CREATIVE WAYS TO DEVELOP PEOPLE

⮌ **Goal: Leverage creative solutions to create growth opportunities outside of promotion**

Creative solutions exist for team members who want to grow (and not just promotions).

Retention increases when people believe they have an opportunity to develop and grow their careers. Most companies have limited options for promotions (only promoting a certain percentage of staff each year, for example). You don't need to offer a promotion to create an opportunity for your team members. Here are strategies to grow your people *without* a promotion.

1. **Initiative assignments.** Initiatives are efforts that have a start date and an end date. Perhaps the company needs help migrating an application, relocating to a new building, or running an off-site company meeting. If one of your people has strong skills to contribute, nominate them to lead initiatives that are compatible with their skill set. This gives them a chance to demonstrate skills they may not showcase in their daily job, like leading a large team. They will also gain exposure to, and familiarity with, other leaders and people in the company, like getting to know the business division managers who will be impacted by the application change. They build their fan club and potential for promotion because those people can give firsthand feedback about their potential and performance.

2. **Leading groups.** Besides leading initiatives, aspiring people managers can develop their skills and stories about leadership in other ways. Ask your aspiring manager to mentor a new hire, speak on a panel to help new college grads, or give written (ideally positive) feedback to other managers about coworkers so she can practice providing specific feedback about strengths to reinforce. You could also encourage your aspiring manager to join a volunteer group in your organization, such as a community outreach group that specializes in tutoring or delivering services to others. Or, have them present a class or workshop on an area of expertise, so they can help others. All these activities count as people leadership on their resume, even if they aren't officially titled as a manager. This work makes a case that when they become a manager, they already have key skills.

3. **Big presentations.** Great managers let their people take credit and present to key stakeholders. If you have a person on your team who aspires to sales leadership, consider inviting them to your next board presentation, and ask them to put together a short part of the presentation (perhaps on the new modeling tool they built to rate sales leads). Before the meeting, do a dry run and have them practice with you. You can coach them on the pace of presentation, content, slide visuals, their confidence and poise, and the like. Their presentation will expose them to the larger context of their work and expose leaders in the company to this person's potential.

4. **Doing more work they love (specializing).** A senior program manager was planning to leave the program team because he wanted to work on tougher, more complicated projects. The team had some projects that aligned with his interests, but protocol dictated that larger projects were evenly distributed, after which smaller projects filled in the gaps. His manager decided to change work assignments so the senior program manager was only in charge of large projects, in addition to setting large program guidelines for other program managers. Once he switched to only doing work he loved (basically creating a new role for him), he stayed with his team and continued doing excellent work for years. He didn't have to seek challenges and growth elsewhere.

5. **Feedback skills.** Feedback isn't something to just focus on with your future management candidates. Growing a culture of feedback within your team means working with everyone on how to share positive and growth-oriented feedback. Even if your team member doesn't aspire to manage others, they are part of a team and should contribute to its growth. Work with your folks on how to frame feedback in a constructive way (specific, actionable) and how to deliver it (in a timely manner, preferably in person).

Most importantly, as you consider developmental assignments as alternatives or paths to promotion, talk to your team member about what you are doing and why. Say, "Miko, I think you have great potential as a people manager, and I know you aspire to it. Would you be willing to take on mentoring Claire when she starts next week? I'd also like to nominate you to the company mentoring pool. What do you think?" Or, "Sean, we have been talking about your career goal to move into sales. The sales team is starting a major software upgrade, and I'd like to recommend you to run this project. It would be a great way to build relationships with the sales team and show them your capabilities. When the project wraps, I bet they will try to bring you onto their team to do long-term support and planning for the platform. What do you think?"

As team members complete the assignments above, make sure you meet with them as the work wraps to talk about what they have achieved. Add notes about their work and results to their performance review, and give them a chance to see what you've written before you commit it to the review system. Take the opportunity to reinforce the point of the work and how this builds their personal brand and provides evidence of their success.

Seeking these creative opportunities *and* explaining their context shows your team members how staying with your team can advance their career. It also shows you care about their development. All without promotions.

MAKE TRAINING IMPACTFUL

Goal: Use the SMART objective structure to increase the impact of training

An underutilized coaching strategy is to maximize training. Whether you suggest training, or your team member signs up for a course on their own, make sure it is as impactful as possible.

When your team member registers for a class or workshop, you have an opportunity to make sure the investment (in terms of money and time) goes beyond the day of training. Consider setting up a SMART objective for your team member. SMART is an acronym that stands for **Specific** (clearly defined), **Measurable** (such that it is black and white about whether the work was completed), **Actionable** (so the person can influence and execute the result), **Realistic** (the expectation is reasonable, given the time and resources), and **Timebound** (it has a deadline and specific date for delivery).

Pairing training with a SMART objective structure might look like this:

- **September 22**—Take Project Management class.
- **By September 29**—Send manager a note identifying a key concept or idea that you will try from the class and what you expect the outcome to be. For example: "I will try to use Gantt charts to visually show timelines, and I expect it will improve clarity between the engineering team and our finance partners."
- **By October 29**—Send manager an email about how things are going, answering the following:
  - *How did you use the Gantt chart, and for whom?*
  - *Did it work as expected? (Better? Worse?)*
  - *Do you think you will use it going forward? Why?*

Too often, people go to training and get inspired, but aren't sure how to leverage what they've learned. Then the content is forgotten over time.

Using SMART guidelines converts taking a class into measurable goals. The person has a responsibility to pay attention, test out a concept, and follow through. It's a great way to reinforce and leverage training.

As a manager, you may also have the opportunity to bring in external trainers for your team, partner with an internal company trainer to support some or all of your team, or leverage online training. No matter the route you take, each type of training benefits from adding applied learning and measuring its effectiveness.

Budgets for Managers

A critical part of management is speaking the objective language of business or "understanding the numbers." This next section doesn't replace business school, but it does cover relevant business budgeting concepts that you might not have learned through previous roles or formal education.

LEARNING FINANCIAL BASICS

➲ **Goal: Learn key numbers for you and your team**

As you are learning, you need to know the *numbers*. Numbers are the objective way organizations and managers measure progress and organizational health. The following worksheet contains questions to ask your boss to help identify important financial concepts and considerations.

This step is part of getting to know the team and the work. Take time to understand your responsibilities around managing your team's budget. When you understand budgeting in a larger context, you see things in a different light. This was true for Mark.

Mark was a new manager at a Fortune 500 company. When he mentioned that his team was far behind on a relocation project, someone suggested bringing in a consulting contractor to do the work. When Mark investigated, he found that the contractor's rates were triple the cost of having an employee do the work. That seemed like a bad solution on the surface.

When he relayed this information to his boss, he got a different perspective. She said the relocation budget was separate from the operating budget. Basically, the relocation costs wouldn't pull from Mark's operating budget, so the contractor wouldn't put his team's budget at risk. Secondly, even though a contractor would cost three times more than an employee, Mark would be able to immediately end the consulting agreement when the move completed. He wouldn't have to find different work for that person, or worry about the costs of a separation package, like he would if that person were an employee. Ultimately, the contractor ended up being less expensive than hiring a new employee would have been. Mark gained a better understanding of budget options and the benefits of using a contractor.

The next worksheet helps you get to know key numbers and their context early on.

Worksheet: Understanding Team Finances

Questions to discuss with your boss to understand the team's finances

Am I responsible for a budget?

Who are my partners in Accounting/Finance/Vendor Management that I can go to with questions?

What are my upcoming budget deadlines (important contract renewals or negotiations, invoice approvals)?

Do we track time in the team for capitalization of labor (something software development and other teams traditionally do)?

If time is tracked, review the tracking/approval system. What are some of the best practices?

Where can I see a list of my team members' salaries, bonus structures, and previous year's ratings?

Are there any current open positions? If so, what is the salary range/organizational band of the position?

When do we make determinations about raises, bonus payouts, and promotions? Can you describe that process and guidelines?

If we have consultants, what are their current budgets/agreements, and how far into the work and spend are we?

PROJECT BUDGETS, KEY TERMS

↻ **Goal: Increase your value by understanding how projects are evaluated from a budget perspective**

When you understand how business leaders evaluate project values and costs, you become an even more trusted and valuable leader. Familiarize yourself with the following key terms:

Payback is the amount of time it takes for a project to start making money. For example, if you build a new mobile application that costs your company $1.5 million and, once launched, it generates $200 thousand a month in new revenue, the payback will happen in 7.5 months. When you understand both the project's cost and the value it will bring, you can make solid recommendations on when a project is expected to be profitable for your company. Some projects will be too expensive to implement because they don't have strong enough results to justify the investment. Others will be critical to prioritize because of their positive payback.

Total cost of ownership (TCO) refers to all costs associated with a product. Perhaps you are planning on implementing a new software tool for your team. The license cost might be $15 per user each month. To fully understand the total cost of using this software though, you have to add in other factors, such as cost to create training, cost to attend training, planned customizations or integrations to other applications, the addition of this tool into your service team's support load, and so on. When you fully understand all the costs related to a project, you can lead your team and others successfully forward.

Gross is a term used for the overall total of something. Net, on the other hand, indicates what is left after deductions. Your paycheck is a simple example, since it shows both total earnings and the actual amount deposited (your earnings minus deductions like taxes, insurance, and social security contributions). These terms are critical for managers to understand a full financial picture. For instance, "gross" might reflect total sales, but if the company is responsible for certain costs (travel expenses, marketing materials) your net profits will be lower.

Sunk costs are costs you can't recover. If your team has worked on building a new software application for six months, and the company changes direction and the application is no longer usable, the time spent building the application is a sunk cost.

Unintended consequences indicate a cost that was unexpected. Perhaps a project resulted in unexpected customer loss, or it caused an increased cost of your data management. Keeping an eye out for unplanned impacts helps you communicate when the payback or TCO are changing.

STAFFING (PAYROLL COSTS)

Goal: Understand how your company assesses the cost of staff

It helps to have background information on how companies assess the cost of staff. A key term to learn is "fully loaded cost." The cost of having an employee is more than just their salary. The fully loaded cost includes things like the company's contribution to healthcare costs, the employee's laptop, workspace, training, and so on. When you understand these, then you fully understand how each additional employee impacts the company budget. Let's use simple numbers to walk through an example.

If Latisha is a project manager on my team and her salary is $100,000 this year, that figure represents only part of her costs to the company. Here are other costs we incur for Latisha:

- Our part of her health insurance coverage
- Our employee 401(k) match
- Her work devices (laptop, cell phone, software licenses)
- Her training (classes or conferences)
- Her professional memberships
- Her personal time off/sick days
- Her workspace (the desk, electrical use, access card, etc.)

Usually, organizations have a way to calculate this. One common estimate is multiplying a person's salary by 1.8 (meaning Latisha's fully loaded cost is $180,000). Figure out what the multiplier is for your company.

Why this matters

Let's say Madeline has a team with a range of experience (and thus a range of pay). Latisha's salary is $100,000, while a few junior folks on the team make $60,000. If Latisha earns an internal promotion to another team, and Madeline has a chance to backfill her position, she might think, "Instead of one senior person, I should hire two junior people." The challenge is to think about costs holistically. If Latisha's true cost is $100K + $80K, and a junior person's true cost is $60K + $48K, one experienced person will cost the company $180K, while two junior people would be $216K.

Two things to keep in mind

1. Fully loaded costs may or may not be how your company accounts for team budgets. Talk to your boss.
2. Two junior people won't necessarily equal one senior.

Most importantly, the best approach is to hire the best talent you can. One very strong person can do the work of multiple average people.

STAFFING (CONTRACTORS)

⮞ **Goal: See how contractors can be an alternative**

Contractors (temporary help paid by the hour) can seem very expensive when compared to employees, but they also can have their place.

Let's say Madeline needs to complete a critical project, and she has to decide if she should hire a new employee or use a contractor. An employee like Latisha costs the company $180K a year (fully loaded cost), while a contractor charging $150 per hour would make $312K a year.

At face value, the employee is the better move. However, hiring a contractor is a good idea (and a lower risk) in situations such as the following:

1. **The project is short term, and you require a subject-matter specialist.** For example, you might hire Darnell the contractor for three months to lead an installation project that won't require ongoing work once completed. Paying Darnell $78,000 is a better decision than hiring a specialist who may not have work after three months, when the project is complete.

2. If the **company has uncertain finances and is worried about layoffs in the future.** If an employee comes on board and you have to let them go six months later, you need to cover their healthcare and pay a severance package. In the time they are employed, you pay for their training, laptops, and vacation days. While a contractor is more expensive, you can separate with them quickly if finances require.

3. Sometimes a contractor's cost can be **affixed to a project**, which can impact the budget differently. A physical relocation of a building or data center, for instance, may have a different budget that could be tied to a contractor, but not an employee.

Keep contractors in mind as an option if you need specialized or short-term help for future projects.

12

Strategic Direction

In this section, the focus is on helping you form strategic direction and discipline for long-term success.

STRATEGY BASICS

Goal: Using insights to build strategy

After a few months in your role, your peers might feel like you have been there forever, and you might be getting overloaded with tactical work. Remember: You are still new AND you are expected to start making a measurable difference. This chapter guides you through those steps.

Work can be classified into two broad categories

1. **Tactical work** involves day-to-day activities. We usually check progress on this work daily, weekly, or maybe quarterly. It is usually urgent and is specific to delivering team results.
2. **Strategic work** involves looking farther out, considering what could go well and what might go wrong, and understanding the implications. It involves big-picture planning for future scenarios.

When you are a manager, you are expected to be on top of both your team's tactical work (what they are doing now) and strategic work (what they may grow to do in the future). It takes a lot of effort to lift yourself from the hard work of the day and think months, or even a year, out. If you are moving from an individual contributor role to a managerial role, you may not be accustomed to deep strategic work. This is a skill that takes practice and must be consciously developed over time.

A manager can fail if they focus on only one area. A tactical-only manager gets work done, but never improves, and may end up leading the team in the wrong direction. A strategic-only manager can fail to deliver by having high-level plans that overlook the reality of daily team management. You need both.

Madeline developed a new personal practice when she was in the third month of her job. Once a month, she would block off a full morning for strategic thinking. She chose a day of the week when she normally felt energized and knew she could think creatively. She would exercise in the morning, and instead of going to her office or hopping on virtual meetings, she went to a coffee shop. There, she set up her laptop, muted all her messaging systems, ordered her favorite tea, meditated, then got to work thinking about strategy.

The mechanics of her setup (a different place, no distractions, and blocks of time) contributed to her ability to think with focus.

This next worksheet covers scheduling a strategy workshop for yourself. You can do this work at home with coffee, at a nook in a bookstore or community workspace, on a park bench—whichever setting helps you concentrate. You could hold a follow-up session with your team, but this initial work is about collecting your thoughts first. Block your time, shut out tactical work and updates, feel comfortable, and breathe. Let's get started.

Worksheet: Manager's Workshop (Strategy)

What are the top goals the company will achieve this coming year? Are there any important dates tied to these goals?

1. _____
2. _____
3. _____

What are key terms we use to describe these goals? (Underline if they appear above or add below. An example: The CEO might mention "speed with intention." How can you bring that language into your team's plan?)

What are five things the team can do to support these top goals?

1. _____
2. _____
3. _____
4. _____
5. _____

Is there any work the team is doing that doesn't fit into these goals? List here:

_____
_____
_____
_____
_____

Take a moment to look at this page. Let's start with the work that doesn't fit. Cross out anything that the team should STOP because it makes no clear contribution to the business and flag anything the team should ADAPT because its contribution to the business is ambiguous.

- Is there anything else the team should STOP doing because it doesn't have a good tie to your goals?
- What adjustments should the team make to ADAPT anything that isn't well aligned to goals?
- Is there anything the team should START doing?

STRATEGY: TEAM GOALS AND MEASUREMENTS

⟳ Goal: Know the WHAT and the MEASUREMENT

Some companies use KPIs (Key Performance Indicators), which are measurements of their strategic goals, or OKRs (Objectives, or business goals, and Key Results), the quantitative measurements used to gauge progress.

Both approaches focus on *objective* and *quantitative* indications of success.

Great managers can:
1. Link their team's work to the context of how the company makes money
2. Demonstrate that they are measuring team performance objectively

Now that you have a sense of your company's strategy and how your team fits into it, let's take the next step and add detail.

Worksheet: Manager and/or Team's Workshop (Team Goals)

This table will help you sketch out team goals. In the bottom row, add any important operational work that needs to happen but may not have a clear connection to team business goals (recruiting a new team member, improving a process, etc.). If you decide to workshop with your team, think about goal-setting or visioning exercises you can do as a group. This big-picture brainstorming energizes people, makes sure everyone is on the same page, and helps everyone feel valued (their input matters!).

COMPANY GOAL / MEASUREMENT / TIMELINE	TEAM GOAL	HOW WE WILL MEASURE SUCCESS	THINGS WE WILL DO NEXT TO SUPPORT THIS GOAL
Key operational work that doesn't tie to growth goals but keeps our company strong:			

After the team has completed the workshop with you, or you have completed this on your own, challenge yourself with these questions:

1. Do I have the right people working on the biggest goals?
2. How am I going to measure my team's contribution? For example, if the primary business goal is to increase traffic on our website, can I list the projects we delivered that support this and use data to explain how we contributed?

STRATEGY: PEOPLE

Goal: Think about your talent strategy

Studies show that highly engaged teams are significantly more productive and profitable than others.[1] How you think about your team is as critical as how you think about the work.

You have made an investment in getting to know your team's strengths. Now, take time to consider how those strengths fit the work. In a perfect situation, you will have a work/person alignment that checks these boxes:

○ Does this work directly support our company's success?

○ Is this person a great fit for this work? Do we expect excellent outcomes?

○ Is there a compelling story here about how this work can potentially advance the person's career and improve well-being?

To do this well, you first need to have a conversation with each team member individually. Then, think about what you have learned about your team overall. The next two worksheets take you through this.

---

1   McKinsey, *Women in the Workplace 2021*, September 27, 2021, https://www.mckinsey.com/-/media/ mckinsey/featured%20insights/diversity%20and%20inclusion/women%20in%20the%20workplace%202021/ women-in-the-workplace-2021.pdf

Worksheet: Career Development Checklist for Team Members

This meeting is supplemental to recurring one-on-ones. To prepare, go back to the discussion you had with your team member about their strengths (or do that step if you haven't had a chance yet).

Building on that information, ask them the following questions:

What percentage of your current work is enjoyable and a great fit for your strengths? Which percentage of your work is not very challenging and fun?

_____
_____
_____
_____
_____

Looking ahead, what role are you ideally doing a year from now? (Is it the same one or something different? Talk about the details of any differences.)

_____
_____
_____
_____
_____

I've noticed [add your observations] about the work you are doing now. Do you agree? (Observations might include whether the person seems to be thriving or whether their current role supports their career aspirations.)

_____
_____
_____
_____
_____

Worksheet: Manager's Workshop (People Strategy)

Everyone has aspects of their work that aren't strategic for their career and might not be much fun. Ideally, most of our responsibilities align with our strengths and, in doing so, set us up for future success, while the hold-our-nose-and-get-it-done part of the job is the minority of the workday.

Before sharing your findings of the previous worksheet with your boss, ask yourself one last question: "If someone asked me if each team member's current day-to-day work is good for their career, would I say yes?" (Keep in mind, you are looking for the majority of their work, not all of it.) Check yourself with the table at the right.

An added benefit of going through this process is recognizing when your team members lack a particular strength that would benefit the group and/or company. When you recruit new people to join your team, keep these opportunities in mind, and hire to fill your gaps.

TEAM MEMBER	WORK ASSIGNED	HOW THIS PLAYS TO THEIR STRENGTHS	WHY THIS IS GOOD FOR CAREER DEVELOPMENT *(or what they will do differently to support their growth)*

STRATEGY: SHOW AND TELL THE STORY

⟳ **Goal: Practice visual storytelling**

The saying, "A picture is worth a thousand words" holds true in the workplace. Pictures are a powerful way to communicate ideas with people and tell a story.

A crucial part of being a manager is telling compelling stories on behalf of the team and their work.

When I led my first multiyear planning process for a big company, I could tell that teams were building plans that were going to conflict with each other in two ways:

- They planned to use the same experts to do work (and needed them during the same weeks), potentially creating delays. For example, each team needed the testing lab at the same time, but the lab could only run one new version of the software at a time, not two.
- They intended to release their applications to the market at the same time, which could overwhelm customers and supply chain partners.

Hot tip!

CONTINUOUS NETWORKING

After your initial flurry of networking, you have probably been focusing so deeply on learning and completing work that you haven't had as many coffees or connections with new people. There seems to be a drop-off in networking during the third month in a new role, and yet it is just as valuable at this point.

This networking fabric is essential to your ability to understand and build strategic plans. To keep building your network fabric, extend new "threads" to other people in your company. Ask your peers who else they recommend you meet or learn from. Attend meetings and send follow-up emails to anyone who catches your interest with their smart or compelling insights.

You are still new, and widening your social circle will help your success.

I experimented with ways to visualize these problems and came up with a timeline that showed application releases with a special visual to show that a lot would happen simultaneously.

Another chart highlighted team resources. I used green to show when projects could be easily staffed and red to show when people would be committed to more than one project.

Free digital tools exist that can give you help with how to share your ideas. You can even use a simple spreadsheet graph. Don't overdesign on your first try. Mock something up and see if one of your coworkers understands the picture without you explaining it.

CHECK-IN ➲ Strategy

You have built on the hard work from your onboarding. You are learning, making adjustments, building plans.

Take a breath. You've made it this far. Let's check in.

Go down the list and summarize what you've accomplished.

- ○ You understand the company strategy.
- ○ You have aligned company goals to team measurements.
- ○ You understand your team's strengths.
- ○ You have considered their strengths and made sure they each have a developmental assignment or work that aligns to their strengths.
- ○ You have rebooted your network and are adding people to your proverbial "boat" who will support your work, your career, and your progress.

Congratulations! Your first months in a new role are complex, challenging, and ultimately rewarding (when you notice your efforts beginning to pay off). Starting to see the full picture and considering the big issues takes a lot of work, but these are crucial investments in your team, your company, and yourself.

13

Performance Management
Feedback and Reviews

By now, you have received reviews from your bosses in other jobs. This section helps you sit on the other side of that process: giving reviews to others and planning their career progression and promotions.

PERFORMANCE REVIEWS

Goal: Understand manager reviews

No matter when you start your role, within the first twelve months, you will be involved in performance reviews.

When I first started managing a team, I worked incredibly hard to prepare for reviews. I wrote very thorough reviews, including for a team member named Elle. Elle's review was three pages long and contained several examples of the things she had done well. She was one of my top performers. My boss insisted that everyone have an area of improvement, so I searched for an idea and lamely put in something about "building leadership presence."

When we met, I spent 44 of our allotted 45 minutes on her strengths and all she had done for us. During the final minute, we talked about "building leadership presence," which I was unable to add much detail to.

For the next six months, Elle worried about her performance. She would anxiously ask me for feedback on how she led meetings and would take minor mistakes very seriously.

I realized I messed up. I made a top performer doubt herself because I followed an outdated notion of performance reviews that expected a section on weaknesses or areas of improvement, even when none came to mind.

The next section is very contrary to what many HR organizations may recommend. This guidance is based on years of experience leading teams. Take what works for you; ignore what doesn't.

Ultimately, how your team performs is a key reflection of YOU. Be open to ideas about how to get the best from them.

YOUR PERSONAL PERFORMANCE REVIEW

Goal: Get your own right

Before we start talking about giving reviews, let's talk about getting your own review right, as a manager.

At a conference I attended, one of the speakers shared a story about a group of women at an investment firm who had lunch together monthly. During one lunch gathering, a few mentioned they had been passed over for a promotion. One woman said, "My boss told me that when the senior leaders were discussing promotions and my name came up, there weren't many stories about me. There were stories about the other people, however, so those people got the promotion."

Make it easy for people to tell your story

Understand that your boss is going to take your self-evaluation and use it as the base of her review.

To begin your self-evaluation, keep a running list of great things you have accomplished. Don't focus on the basic parts of your job (doing reports, running meetings, hiring people), but instead highlight the high-impact parts of your work (your team's early delivery of a project, a new process that cut costs by 15 percent, how you raised your team's engagement scores and their results went up by 4 percent). It's critical that you wrap your team's success in the summary of yourself.

Reinforce the achievements that underscore your unique skills.

Reinforce your team accomplishments and your role in making them happen.

Tell these accomplishments as stories: "Our refund rates from the site were 33 percent, so I led the team through a discovery process. Aisha and Brent figured out that we have a problem with fine print. Bea and Juan suggested we add a pop-up to show available dates as a step in the purchase. We normally take three months to make similar changes, but by using paired programming, we delivered in six weeks. Since then, refund rates have dropped to 10 percent, driving a monthly revenue impact of $250,000. We reached that outcome through a combination of research, creative programming, and measuring our work."

Next, repurpose your self-evaluation stories to talk about yourself. If the CEO sees you in the hallway and asks how you are doing, reply with something like, "Great. My team delivered the software release two weeks early due to some changes we made in our testing process." Always have a story ready about yourself. Stories stick in people's minds, and those stories will be retold in talent roundtable discussions about your performance.

Worksheet: Accomplishment Tracking, Self

At the beginning of the year, block time in your calendar at the end of each quarter to catch up on your list of accomplishments.

Use the guide below to track your accomplishments (or keep an electronic version so you can easily add it to a self-review document).

ACCOMPLISHMENT	HOW THE OUTCOME WAS MEASURED	WHY IT'S IMPORTANT TO THE COMPANY

REVIEWING YOUR TEAM

⟳ Goal: Get your team's written reviews right

This section focuses on your reviews of your team.

If you enter performance reviews into an HR system, I recommend writing them in a document first and starting early. It's helpful to draft them, let them sit for a few days or a week, then come back to them. If you have managers who work for you, ask them to do the same so you can review together before they go into the system.

Be brief and specific

As a manager, you will find yourself reviewing three types of people (generally speaking), and the reviews you deliver for each will be very different.

- **Poor performers.** These reviews are usually written in partnership with HR. In this scenario, you don't believe this person has the capacity for improvement. The focus here is on documentation that supports the likely decision to let them go in the near future.

- **Top performers.** Top performers need nearly full encouragement and recognition. Recognize specific instances of exceptional performance, encourage the person to build on their skills, and deemphasize or set aside negatives.

- **Average performers.** The most challenging review to write is for average performers who have the potential to improve, but are struggling in some areas. You'll want to review these performers in a way that provides a balance of corrective feedback and encouragement.

The following sections cover these three types and give you a basis to approach these very different situations.

Worksheet: Poor Performer Review Checklist

If you want or need to let someone go because they are performing badly, your goal is to set the stage for a smooth exit. A poor performer drags the rest of the team down. Documentation is critical here, and your HR partners (and possibly the legal team) need to be involved to help make sure things are both fair and actionable.

You need to write their performance reviews with these elements:

○ Use specific examples of problems and, more importantly, the days you discussed these issues with them, and how the issues have recurred. You can't surprise someone with performance problems in a review. Undiscussed performance issues aren't their failure; they're yours as their manager. Use your in-the-moment coaching and follow up with emails. Then tie those to the review.

○ Be empathetic, while being fair, firm, and specific.

○ Give explanations of why these examples are problematic for the company (they create quality problems, cause delays, etc.).

○ Work with HR. Have them review what you've written and agree to support the start of the exit process.

Worksheet: Top Performer Review Checklist

If the person you are reviewing is a **top performer and a significant contributor to your team**, do none of the previous section. You want them to **stay and continue to improve**.

Schedule their review well in advance, on one of the first days HR says reviews can be conducted (even top performers are nervous waiting for their reviews). Send a copy of the review in advance so they can read it through before you meet.

Use the following practices when conducting their performance review:

○ Provide specific examples of what they have done well and why it matters to you and the company. This reinforces good behavior and hopefully encourages them to do more of the same.

○ Reinforce their self-evaluations. Say things like, "In your personal assessment, you said you have helped the data team turn the corner, and I completely agree." Let them feel heard.

○ Give feedback from their peers and relevant customers. Hearing from multiple voices helps validate and empower staff. If someone provides feedback for your team member that you think is inaccurate or nonproductive, edit it out. There might be one grouchy person whose feedback was based on their own bad day. Don't blow up a person's self-esteem for an outlier. When I solicit feedback from others, I ask things like, "What does Kate do that makes her uniquely valuable to the project team?" Or, "Are there things Kate should do more or less often to be even more impactful?"

○ Include a statement about their strengths and how they can build on those strengths to grow their career. Seriously consider giving them no negative feedback.

○ Tell them they are making a difference and positively impacting the company.

○ Start strong and end strong, and say thank you.

Worksheet: Average Performer Review Checklist

If the person you are reviewing is an **average member of your team**, you need a hybrid approach. You want to give them **a clear chance to improve, be motivated to change, and stay**.

Make sure you have been meeting with this person in advance of the review; they shouldn't be surprised by the content of your discussion, especially in regards to their shortcomings. Send a copy of the review in advance so they can read it through before you meet.

In preparing this review, keep these points in mind:

○ Tell them why you believe in them and how you have confidence that they can turn the situation around.

○ Provide specific examples of what they have done well and why it matters to you and the company. This reinforces good behavior and hopefully encourages them to do more of the same.

○ Provide specific examples of areas in which they are struggling, and discuss clear action plans and measurements to improve, including target dates. Set target dates for the next three months, so there is a clear path to improvement.

○ Reflect on their self-evaluations. Speak to their awareness of the challenges, or their lack of awareness.

○ Give feedback from their peers and relevant customers. Hearing from multiple voices helps give the person an understanding of who will be involved in the improvement process. When I solicit feedback from others for a person who is struggling, I ask questions like, "Are there things Pat should do to improve his outcomes for you and your team?"

○ Reiterate why you know they can improve, that their improvement is something within their control, and that you are invested in helping them succeed.

○ Ask for their feedback and look for signs of commitment. Set the next step in the process.

○ Say thank you.

A Coaching Success Story

Developing your team can take a lot of work, and you have to understand your goal as you work with someone.

Amy started on Madeline's team in a consultant role and fit in with the team immediately. However, she did not immediately fit in with her role. She struggled throughout her first quarter and into the next. She was open to feedback and worked alongside Madeline to try multiple ideas: a peer mentorship with another newer team member, a working session with a senior member of the team, daily check-ins with Madeline to prioritize her workload. By the fourth month, Amy and Madeline reached the same conclusion: this role was not a fit for Amy, but Amy was a great fit for the organization.

Madeline felt strongly that Amy was still an asset to the department. She came up with a solution, and after consulting with HR and her director, she proposed her idea to Amy. Amy could transition to an associate project management role on the team, and then perhaps change teams as she grew (and the need for an associate project manager arose elsewhere). Madeline felt Amy was detail-oriented, very dependable, and personable. Amy was interested and excited by the idea. Madeline advocated for the role change and got it approved. Amy accepted and shifted into the project management role shortly after.

Within the next month, Madeline received a call from Taylor, the VP of the infrastructure team. Taylor said, "I hear Amy is awesome and open to learning. What are the chances you'd be willing to let her transfer to my team in an operations coordinator role?"

Madeline realized that her advocacy had built a brand for Amy, distinguishing her as someone who'd jump into a challenge. Madeline told Taylor she would talk with Amy and follow up.

When Amy heard about the offer, she was excited, but nervous. She asked Madeline, "Do you think I'm qualified?"

Madeline told her, "If we were friends through other circumstances, I'd tell you to take it. It's a new role on a quickly growing team and a great opportunity. Plus, it's flattering that you're being poached!"

Amy accepted the new role and was thriving within two months. As an added bonus, when Madeline's team needed urgent support from Amy's new team, they received help quickly from their former coworker and her new team members.

ORGANIZATION-LEVEL TALENT REVIEWS

⟳ **Goal: Understand talent reviews and tools**

Many companies have mechanisms for creating fairness in scoring and promoting staff. Learn how to use these for your own purposes and in talent reviews.

First: Roundtable Meetings

After a ratings period (usually at the end of the year or midyear), managers from across teams may come together in a roundtable meeting. As a group, they go through talent at a particular level. To achieve this, the company may compile a merged list of all teams and their performance ratings (after each manager has rated their own individuals). As the group looks at the list of all the staff at a particular level, the managers are invited to comment and asked if they have observations. Someone might say, "I am surprised Horatio is rated so low. He did a great job on Project X this year." Or, "I am surprised Anna is rated so high. This group has talked about her challenges with on-time delivery."

- Sometimes you discover that one manager is a harder grader than others, and the group will decide to increase someone's rating.
- Sometimes you discover that a manager has a blind spot for one of their employees.
- At times, you find that when you line up all the top-ranked people at a particular level, it becomes obvious who does and doesn't fit there.

Here are key ways for you to contribute and prepare for a roundtable and score calibration:

1. Come prepared with brief explanations for why you rated each of your people as you did. You might write something like, "Fatima delivered the Agile Maturity model and the new pricing program on time and is well regarded by all the engineering managers."
2. Bring examples and specific stories of employees on other teams with whom you've interacted. You may want to advocate for a higher score or provide justification for a lower score.
3. Be brief, be specific.
4. Bring notes.
5. Don't share the conversations outside the doors.
6. Most importantly, advocate for your team.

Second: Stack Ranks

Beyond the roundtable, you can use other mechanisms, such as stack ranks, to create fairness in scoring and promoting staff.

In this exercise, list your staff from most valuable to least valuable. This is a private list, and you shouldn't share it. Honestly, when you have ushered poor performers from the company, and your whole team is composed of top performers, it's difficult to write this list. At some point your company may have to have layoffs. You need this list handy.

Even if you don't have layoffs, it is helpful to understand how your team members rank on the list and consider how you should treat each person.

- For your top folks: Are you sure they enjoy their jobs and will stay? Invest time in them, making sure they have work that suits their interests and talents.
- For your middle folks: Have you given them work that allows them a chance to stretch and grow—work that interests them? (Sometimes middle folks like the comfort of the middle. See the section about how not everyone wants career growth for more on this topic.)
- For your bottom folks: Confirm if their position is due to inexperience, quality of work, or other variables. Make sure they have appropriately assigned work and support. People working on performance issues should be second to last. The people in your poor performer/need-to-leave-the-organization category are at the bottom of the list.

Lastly: Nine Blocks or Ready Ratings

Another handy review tool is the Nine Block. A Nine Block is composed of nine categories that indicate a person's readiness for promotion in terms of potential and performance. Place your team member into the square that fits them best (see below). Another simpler version around promotion is to categorize each team member as either Ready Now, Ready Short-Term, or Ready Long-Term.

Potential:
The ability to assume increasingly broad or complex responsibilities as business needs change during the next 12–18 months

Performance:
The extent to which an individual can deliver results, demonstrate competencies, and act in spirit of company values

↑ POTENTIAL

• Focus on coaching • Provide develop plan • Concerned with lack of motivation **DEVELOP**	• Valuable team member • Room for performance improvements • Challenge them **DEVELOP / STRETCH**	• Has mastered current role • Provide new assignments that stretch and push their skills • Future leader **STRETCH**
• Shows potential, but performance is low • Focus on skills to improve performance • Consider PIP **OBSERVE**	• Consider increasing responsibilities • Meeting current expectations • Create development plan **DEVELOP**	• Exceeding performance expectations • Identify skill gaps for probable promotion, and develop those skills **STRETCH / DEVELOP**
• Not meeting performance expectations • Upskill needed or find new role **OBSERVE / EXIT**	• Consistent contributor, but limited potential • Put on performance improvement plan • Might need a successor **OBSERVE**	• Strong performer but unlikely to move to higher-level role • Will need motivation to stay engaged **DEVELOP**

PERFORMANCE →

Table originally created by McKinsey & Company

14

Interviewing & Hiring

As your team grows and evolves,
finding and onboarding talent is critical.

JOB DESCRIPTION BASICS

⊃ **Goal: Define what you need**

The first step in hiring is to make sure the job description you post and share will attract the person you want. Before you casually repost a job description from the past, read it over carefully. The work, as well as what customers and the business needs, usually evolves and changes over time. Take the time to evaluate an existing job description and make sure it reflects your current needs.

Your first hires are a critical way for you to influence how the team expands or how you replace someone who left. The following guide can help you organize your plan before the search begins.

It starts with thinking about your team. What have you learned about key behaviors and values that are most important to your success? At McDonald's, people often used the phrase "An Ace in Place." This term referred to a superstar restaurant employee who was so good at their job that a smaller team could be scheduled when they worked because the Ace could essentially perform the work of several employees. I'm sure you have seen this in your own career—a project manager who is so good, she can carry one-and-a-half times as many projects as other project managers, or a finance person who finishes their quarter financial close analysis in half the time of others. These people create significant results for their teams and their companies.

Hiring gives you the opportunity to find your next Ace in Place.

Worksheet: Writing Job Descriptions

First Step: Check in on what it is you need from this new person at this time

1. Gather your thoughts. Find a quiet moment. Ask yourself:

a. What do I need most from this person?

b. What work am I likely to assign to this person?

c. Which teams or people will work with this person?

d. Since the role was last filled (assuming this is a backfill), what have I learned about the role that might lead to revisions in the past job description?

e. Is there anything important to avoid as we evaluate candidates?

f. If I hire well, what will that person accomplish in the next year that will clearly indicate that I filled the role well?

Second Step: The job description itself

Before you start writing a brand-new job description, there is a high chance one already exists. It may include language that is critical to your company (and saves you work). Find a copy of the existing one, and consider if it fits as is or if anything needs adjusting.

2. Read the description and edit. Areas to check include:

- Is the job description written for the proper seniority level? Do you need it to be more senior? If so, talk to your boss about how that might impact the budget. Could the role be filled by someone more junior? If so, that might make recruitment a bit easier. Adjust the description based on the experience level you need.

- Is there language in the description that is out of date? (Perhaps you now use a new tool for managing work, but the old tool is still listed.)

- Are the "must-haves" in the required section true? If not, they might rule out great candidates. Keep in mind that non-diverse candidates are more inclined to apply for jobs if they only meet part of the requirements. Diverse candidates, on the other hand, tend to only apply for jobs if they meet ALL requirements.

- Look closely at the educational background and experience. Do you need both? Can you use language like "a degree in X or commensurate experience"?

- Now, the most important part: Do the top paragraph and bullet points convey a clear, exciting message to attract the Aces you want? Can you shorten them? Can you reorder bullet points so critical job elements are at the top?

- Do a quick search for language that has unintended social bias. Find a recent article or research project that describes words with unintended social bias, and check your job description for those words. These words can exclude or discourage diverse candidates and should be modified to be more inclusive before posting.

Third Step: Partner with your boss and HR to complete the description
You have a solid draft, you have thought through the important elements, and you can explain your suggested changes. Talk to your boss and your Human Resources partner to finalize the description before you post it and start the search. Consider having a diverse group of employees weigh in on the language in the description.

3. Finalize the description. Areas to review with HR and your boss:

○ Walk through your suggested changes and your thoughts behind them. Discuss any refinements.

○ Have any of your changes altered the appropriate salary band or level? (A salary band is the range of compensation for a particular role in a company. Usually, a job description will have an ideal low and high end for pay. This allows top performers to be paid more than emerging talent. When the person is eventually promoted, they will shift into the next band.)

Hot tip!

WHY DIVERSITY ON YOUR TEAM CAN CONTRIBUTE TO SUCCESS

Studies from research organizations, including Gallup, show that groups with diverse educational and personal backgrounds solve problems more effectively than homogenous groups.[1] Evaluate your team with fresh eyes. Are you all highly experienced? Are you all the same gender? The same race or ethnicity?

People experience the world through different lenses. Recognize that adding someone whose race/gender/sexual orientation/abilities are different than most of the team's will bring a new perspective, perhaps reflective of your customers or partners. Deliberately add these lenses/perspectives to your team. When your team sees the world from different angles, they will likely ask more questions, consider multiple approaches, and solve problems more effectively, for both your team and your organization.

---

1 Gallup, *State of the Global Workplace: 2022 Report,* https://www.gallup.com/workplace/349484/ state-of-the-global-workplace-2022-report.aspx.

FINDING PEOPLE
⟲ Goal: Find strong talent

In most companies, a talent acquisition team will post your job position, review resumes, and forward names to you that seem to be a good fit. In many cases, these teams are overwhelmed with work and have talent pipelines they consistently use. It may take a while to find the kind of talent you need to fill your role with an Ace.

Become an active contributor to the talent pipeline by doing the following:

1. **Connect to others through social media, especially people who are different from you.** When you are at any kind of gathering, especially industry events, connect with people through your online networking platforms. Include a note with your invitation to connect ("Emma, really enjoyed your talk on green energy," "Andre, so nice to connect in the workshop on hybrid learning"). When you do this, you leave a small reminder of the context of how you met. If you don't interact for a while, your message history will serve as a handy reminder of how you met and what impressed you about them. These people will see your posts about open positions, or they could help you learn about other candidates.

2. **Pay attention inside your company.** When someone mentions another person who is "so smart" or "a real top performer" or any other compliment you think is interesting, reach out and invite that person to an informal coffee (virtual or otherwise). Simply chat, and get to know them. It could be that in the months ahead, you may have an open position they are suited for, or they may be able to recommend someone else.

3. **Pay attention to your own team.** Is there someone who might want to change roles or take on harder work? If so, you have the advantage of already being familiar with this individual and their work. If you think they'd be a good fit, this could be a win for both of you.

Worksheet: Learn About the Posting and Interview Process

You have the job description, and you have been building your pipeline of talent. Now, the interview process starts. Begin with the following two steps:

1. Ask your HR or talent acquisition partner if there are data entry steps you need to complete to get the position posted. Perhaps you have to submit a position request in your HR system, or step through an automated approval process.
2. Review the standard interview process. In the following chart, add the steps for your organization (the first two rows contain examples). Make notes about whether you need to write entries in a system, add interview scores, etc.

STEP	PERSON RESPONSIBLE	GOAL	NOTES
Phone Screening	*Marta in Talent Acquisition*	*Figure out potential fit and candidate interest.*	
Initial Manager Phone Screening	*You*	*Informally get to know candidates. Talk about role, ask initial questions to assess fit. Determine if someone should progress to the next step.*	

Hot tip!

INCREASE SUCCESS FOR DIVERSE AND/OR EXPERIENCED CANDIDATES

If you interview young diverse candidates, they have different challenges than young non-diverse candidates. They may not have had access to internships or mentors who could coach them through interviewing. As a result, the mechanics of interviewing may be an obstacle for them.

On the other hand, if you are interviewing a very experienced person, this person will probably have interviewing mechanics down. They are likely to make a decision based on different factors, including organizational, culture, or value fit.

A similar mechanism can help both. Consider an informal coffee or meeting with the candidate before the interview process starts.

When a diverse candidate has an early, informal visit to see the office, become familiar with the building location, and get to know the check-in process, etc., they will feel better prepared for the interview day. This familiarization can help alleviate stress and build initial confidence.

When an experienced candidate has an informal conversation or visit before interviews, you can share the case for working for you and with your team. You can also give them a glimpse of your office's culture by visiting an area reflective of the teams with whom they will interact. This can sell a more experienced candidate on considering the position.

In both cases, you set candidates up for success.

INTERVIEWING WITH MULTIPLE INTERVIEWERS

Strengthen your interview outcomes by involving others

You know the process details now. You know what you need. You have a great job description.

Now it's time to invite people who are critical to your team's success into the boat with you. There is an old saying, "No one drills a hole in the bottom of a boat they are sitting in." If you include others you trust in your interview process, they will have a vested interest in supporting your candidate when the candidate starts. Interviewers who could fall into this category include experienced managers, individual contributors from other teams who will work frequently with the new hire, or high performers on your team who understand the role well.

Your HR team may have specific interview guidelines, such as how separate interviews are recommended or if a panel is used (multiple people from your company meeting with one candidate at the same time). If not, you can build your own plan.

Best practices to consider:

1. Hold a briefing meeting before the interviews start

Organize your thoughts and create a pre-brief document and meet with your interviewers. Review the following areas:

a. The role that needs to be filled.

b. Who the new hire will replace and why (for new roles, discuss why it is necessary to add this position).

c. What you believe is most important (and an example of someone doing well in this role, if you have one).

d. What, specifically, you need each person to look for and why. This is critical. You don't want a project manager to assess a finance person's business acumen, but you could ask, "Do you feel this person would be a good partner on technology projects?" You don't want a grouchy technologist to decide if the person is "a cultural fit," but you would like to hear their opinion on the person's depth of technical knowledge.

e. Questions you suggest or request they use.

f. If the interview has multiple interviewers, cover how to split up the time, how you will take turns asking questions, and who will open and close the interview.

g. Explain timing (their interview length, when they need to submit feedback).

h. Say thank you. This is hard work, and they are going to help you make a great decision.

2. Request written feedback from interviewers about each candidate interview

Their feedback can be shared with others as you make a final decision about hiring.

3. Request the feedback and score, if applicable, go directly to HR or to you

This way, the interviewers don't influence each other in advance of their conversations. The score can be as simple as: hire, maybe, don't hire.

4. Debrief as a group

Ideally, HR will facilitate the debrief, but you can as well. Ask each person to share their feedback and score.

5. Determine action

If there is disagreement about whether to hire or not, and you feel the candidate should still be considered, do one of two things:

a. Arrange another interview to dig in deeper on the issue/area of concern.

b. Or, if you feel the candidate is a good fit and the observation is an outlier, let the interviewer know you are moving forward, explain why, and ask for their help to monitor the new hire. (Keep them in the boat.)

6. After an offer is extended, send a note to interviewers . . .

a. Saying thank you.

b. Asking them to reach out via email or social media to welcome the person to the company. Start building that network for your new team member early, and help keep your interviewers involved in the person's long-term success.

INTERVIEW QUESTIONS

⟳ **Goal: Choose interview questions that give insight and make for a positive interview experience for the candidate**

Consider splitting the following questions between your interviewers, so folks can ask questions that focus on their particular area of assessment.

Questions for all roles

- Talk about a time when stakeholders didn't see eye to eye with each other or with you. What was your solution?
- What risks have you taken, and what have you learned?
- Tell me about a mistake you made and what you learned from it.
- Tell me about a time you lacked the skills or knowledge to achieve a goal.
- What is your top strength?
- What is your weakness, and what are you doing to improve it?
- When was the last time you were happy at work?
- When was the last time you were ticked off at work?
- Which of your past roles was the best fit?
- Tell me about a time you had a disconnect with your leader.
- What is a criticism you have received during your career?
- How do you assess whether you will fit into an organization?
- Tell me about a time you had to deal with a tough customer.

Questions for leaders/managers

- Describe your leadership style.
- Are you more effective in a group or one-on-one?
- Tell me about a time you had a tough conversation, including the outcome.
- What do you like most about managing people?
- What is difficult about being a leader?
- Tell me about a time when you helped a team member make an adjustment so they could get better at their job.
- How do you manage poorly performing employees?
- How do you gain commitment from a team?
- Tell me about a time you took leadership without authority.
- How do you build consensus?
- Tell me about a time you had to build a strategy for your team.
- How can we help you succeed as a leader?
- What one word describes you as a leader?

15

Onboarding People

When you onboard people, your goal is to immediately create a sense of belonging and purpose.

ONBOARDING NEW HIRES SUCCESSFULLY

○ **Goal: Help folks come up to speed as positively and quickly as possible**

Everyone is nervous about the first day. Even if you are an expert in your field, a new job means you have new people to meet, new technology to learn, and new processes and work context to figure out.

Create a welcome packet (or adjust your company's existing template, if possible). It's helpful to provide a 90-day onboard plan for your new hire. For the first week, make sure they have four things:

1. Technology and access to systems and relevant resources
2. Friendly people to meet each day that can answer their questions
3. Time to think (everyone needs a chance to process what they have learned)
4. A plan for the first three months

If they are junior, your plan needs to include information about how to do their job. If you can list classes they can schedule on their own, research they can read in their free time, etc., you will give them a sense of autonomy and purpose.

If they are senior, balance your onboarding with connecting them to great people (and relationship-building opportunities) and providing research and information to help them succeed.

A checklist for successful onboarding follows.

Hot tip!

WHY MULTIPLE ONBOARDING BUDDIES MAKES SENSE

If you want to onboard a person successfully, give them an onboarding buddy. Heck, give them four.

Why four? Of the four buddies you choose, there is a good chance at least one will form a long-lasting friendship with your new hire. Additionally, if one of the buddies doesn't work out, there are others to lean on. Consider assigning someone from your team to be a first-two-weeks buddy (covering how to find coffee, use tech, and other basics). The second buddy could be a person from your team who has the same role and can field any work questions. The third could be an individual from a different business group. Lastly, the fourth could be a manager who is not the person's manager.

Worksheet: Onboarding Checklist

This plan (and the elements below) will help your new hire survive and thrive.

- ○ Equipment and access all set
- ○ 90-day onboarding plan written

Confirm this 90-day plan includes:

- ○ List of people to schedule conversations with and why. This lets the person contact someone and say, "My new manager suggested I reach out to you. She says you are the expert in our Marketing tech stack." Or, "My boss suggested I reach out to you for a virtual coffee. She said you have a great reputation for on-time projects, and I'd love to learn more about what you believe makes someone effective here." The new team member now has context to add a note to the invitation that both flatters the recipient (building a relationship and enhancing your relationship with the person) and explains the context for the meeting.

- ○ List of multiple "onboarding buddies." This way, if one isn't the best fit personality wise, another might be. Consider: a peer, a person in a different team at a similar level, a manager or leader in another team, a business or technical person who can shed light on a key group your team partners with, and so on.

- ○ List of classes to take and research to complete. With this list, a new person can begin self-learning on their own time and pace.

- ○ A schedule of key events. Confirm they have key team meetings on their calendar. Make sure they know the date of big company meetings as well.

- ○ Make sure they have someone to connect with each day during the first two weeks—perhaps for lunch—so they don't feel alone.

- ○ Expectations of work over the first 90 days, including key tasks to accomplish and how you will measure success.

- ○ Vital contact information to get help.

- ○ Scheduled end-of-day check-ins for at least the first two weeks. Encourage the new hire to keep a running list of questions for you, so you can resolve any issues quickly. This is also a clear sign of your interest in their success.

Situational Manager Tools

This section includes insightful modules and tools to help you with situations most managers experience. Team management isn't a talent people are born with. Team management skills are learned and shared.

This section provides tools, exercises, and advice for situations that can arise. Consider skimming through this section once to become aware of the resources, and return to it when the situations present themselves.

Many managers have wonderful bosses who pull them into their workspace and say things like, "Hey, the talent roundtable/team offsite/holiday party is coming up, let's talk about how you might approach this." The goal of this section is to recreate that sense of focused advice for when you need it.

Imagine you are having coffee or tea with Christine and Madeline, and we are giving you the inside scoop. When you get insider guidance from others, you are likely to avoid common missteps that can happen when you do something new. In turn, avoiding these missteps can help accelerate your career. This guide's goal is to help you move quickly and accurately, so you are lined up for more opportunities in the future.

How to Recharge

How do you "refill your cup" when your energy is low?

Sanity List

Set aside your daily plan and your work. With a clean page in front of you, ask yourself, "What is bugging me? Are there things (personal, workwise) that distract me because I have been putting them off?" Tasks that seem small (put suitcases away from trip) or big (get tax information together) can distract you and drain energy. Make a list of things that would make you sane and add tidiness to your general existence. Then do them.

Household Help

A cleaning service can help you by shouldering part of your domestic obligations and giving you a clean place to think, sleep, and be. Oddly, clean sheets have been noted as improving sleep—even a small thing like this can help.

Amy Cuddy's Power Pose

Check out the TED Talk from Amy Cuddy.[1] Two minutes of standing straight with your hands on your hips and breathing evenly can help you recharge.

Exercise (consider bicycling or running)

We know how exercise can quiet the mind and build strength. When you run, bike, or walk, you sense progression as you pass things. That imagery can help you look forward to your day.

Meditation and Journaling

Especially in the morning, consider a practice of meditation or journaling to start your day well.

Carve Out Quiet Time

Set aside time to reflect, think, and plan. Calendars can get hectic. Reserve time in your calendar for white space or quiet moments to think about what has happened and what is coming.

Take a Day Off, and Really Disconnect

Your team needs a good role model for how to take time off and recharge, and the best role model is you. Schedule time off, and really unplug. Set notifications to let anyone who contacts you know that you are unavailable. Don't check messaging systems. Clear your mind of work and focus on something else that is important to you.

Remember, You Chose This

We choose our paths for different reasons. If your workload is heavy right now, say to yourself, "I chose this job because I wanted a challenge." If you are feeling worried about preparing for a big presentation, remind yourself, "I want to be a leader, and I choose to take this on to improve my leadership communication." When you remind yourself that things aren't happening to you, but rather, you sought them out, that can help you rebuild energy.

---

1 Amy Cuddy, "Your Body Language May Shape Who You Are," TEDGlobal (2012), https://www.ted.com/talks/amy_cuddy_your_body_language_may_shape_who_you_are.

Work Parties

Presence and professionalism are important at what may seem to be just a social gathering.

Work parties are a critical part of leadership. Even if you aren't a party person, you need to attend to show your support of your team, your company, and your coworkers. Keep the following strategies in mind:

A copilot. When you attend these parties with a friend or your partner, have them be your copilot. Before you go, say, "If we come up to someone and I don't immediately introduce you, could you shake hands and say, 'I'm Mitchell,' so they have to reply with their name?" This is a great tactic to use when you are still working on recalling names.

Strategic greetings to your team and others. Let's say you see Juliet from your team, and she is with her partner Beth. After saying hello, turn to Beth and say something like: "I can't tell you how much we appreciate Juliet here. She made a huge difference for us during our last release." These introductions can be a moment to appreciate each staff person individually, recognize that their partner might have to give up time with them so they can work for you, and put positive energy into the night.

Drinking. Carry a drink with you, but, ideally, don't drink while you are at the event (consider carrying a seltzer water with a lime slice as an option). You need all your wits about you. Even if everyone says this is a social event and there will be no work talk, your personal relationships are what will support your career progression. Also, you are a manager, and in a worst-case scenario, you might need to look out for your folks.

A plan. Yes, it's a party. But it's a work party. Before you go, think about who you'd like to see and what you want to talk about. Do you want to ask Marco how his son's broken arm is healing? Or ask Mia about her trip to Montreal? Or tell LaDonna she did a great job solving the bug in the last release? Or tell the president how much you are enjoying her new weekly update? Going in with a plan will alleviate some of the pressure to improvise each interaction.

C-Level Aspiration, Game Plan

You want to be a C-level leader. Here are tools to help you seek the insight you need to chart your course.

Here are three things great CXOs (CEO, COO, CIO, and others) are capable of and how you can take action to demonstrate these capabilities:

Creating and communicating strategy
Action: Consider building decks/slides to show your ideas to others (and use friends outside your company to do reviews/provide feedback). This works well when you have come up with a new idea and are hoping to build support for it. Before you show your presentation to your final audience, test-drive it with others first, sharing your approach and welcoming suggestions for improvement.

Showing progress through numbers
Action: Make sure you are using numbers to communicate your progress on goals (we were at X, my team did 123 work, now we are at Z). You might have to provide a weekly status report, or, perhaps, someone will ask you to send a message with a progress summary. These are great opportunities to use objective numbers to show progress.

Making decisions and seeking consensus
Action: C-level leaders need to make decisions and seek consensus. Discussion documents can help you build consensus and test-drive a decision with others. Put together no more than one page to share with someone from whom you need coaching, a decision, or guidance. The discussion document could contain an option A/option B summary, a pros and cons list, a rough mock-up of an organization design you want to implement—whatever captures your ideas and the problems you are facing. Keep it brief, don't strive for perfection, and use bullet points. Put the question/goal you want to discuss at the top ("I'd like your feedback on my challenge with the org redesign," or "I am inclined to choose option A over B. Would appreciate your input"). Writing these notes will help you prepare for the conversation and show your thought process. This approach also helps you make sure you have fully considered the challenge before you bring others into the conversation. As you share this discussion document with others, you will build support for your ideas and consensus about next steps.

In addition to the above actions you can take in your current role, you can interview someone who is currently in the role you aspire to.

Ask people to help you find a CXO who might be willing to have coffee with you (virtual or in person) for half an hour to talk about their career. When you make the connection, either have your person introduce you, or send a note saying, "I asked Jill who would be a good person to connect with for coffee, and she recommended you. I'm considering my own career planning and would appreciate hearing about your path to your role. Thanks so much for considering."

If the conversation goes well, ask the CXO if they would be willing to follow up with you in a month or so as you build your career development plan. If it only went okay, or you don't feel a connection, just say thank you. You still got what you needed!

Your conversation with the CXO should give you great clues about their path. As they talk about the day/quarter/year in a life, does the job still sound like something you want? As they share their insight, do you feel clarity about what you can do to build experiences that are relevant to this career path? In particular, pay attention to the change between the CXO's former role to their current one, and ask them what surprised them. What you learn from this question can help prepare you for future interviews and instruct you on how to articulate your readiness to take on the role's challenges.

Sample questions to ask:

- Looking back, what experiences did you complete that positioned you for successful promotion and best prepared you for this role?
- Who helped you on your path, and is there someone similar you could recommend who might help me?
- As you think about successful CXOs, what do you think are the top three criteria for a successful CXO?
- Can you talk me through a quarter in the life, or a year in the life, of a CXO? Where do you spend most of your time? What are the most critical things you focus on during the day/quarter/year?
- What was the biggest change from your previous role to this one?
- What surprised you as you shifted into this role?
- Did you have mentors who helped guide you to this role? What did they do that was most helpful?
- How did you establish mentors once you stepped into this role, and what support has been the most helpful?
- Is there anyone else you recommend I connect with?

Innovation Leader

Workshopping ideas and getting creative with others can lift your spirits. It can also lift your company's revenue.

Managers are expected to be idea people who inspire their teams to think differently! Find solutions! Discover breakthroughs!

Here is the secret: Great ideas won't necessarily come from you, they will come from your people who are closest to your market, your customers, and the product. You need to set the stage. Here are ideas to spark innovative thinking:

1. **Set up in a different place**—a co-working space or an out-of-office retreat. It's easier to think differently when your setting is different.

2. **Let your teams run experiments.** Support your folks when they're coming up with ideas and figuring out how to measure them. Let them go for a few weeks. Consider even the most far-fetched ideas, but use good boundaries when it comes to time and measurement.

3. **Budget for unknowns.** Reserve dollars and time in your plans for any unknowns that may crop up next year. This will give you space to, say, buy a software tool, purchase equipment that supports a short-term test, or make a trip to test out an idea. Leave space for the unplanned.

4. **Advocate for your team** to share their ideas and results with senior leaders and other teams in the company. People will be excited about showcasing their progress, and your team will build its brand as an innovative group in the company.

Stay Interview

Retention is crucial. The Stay Interview is a great tool to help you keep your best people.

Twice a year (I put this as a recurring meeting on my calendar with my team leaders), ask your people these questions:

What are you doing now that you enjoy most?
Here you are listening for clues about how they might be evolving and where they are most engaged in their work.

If you had to guess the percentage of your job you enjoy versus the percentage you don't, what is your breakdown?
If your person says they enjoy 70 percent or more of their work, while 30 percent or less is not quite as fun, that's a good sign. If they enjoy less than 70 percent of their work, talk together about whether there is a chance to improve the balance. Less interesting tasks could, perhaps, be delegated to someone who enjoys that work, or project assignments could be rebalanced. There will always be unenjoyable parts of a person's job that they need to push through, but when you increase the parts that are interesting and rewarding, it helps that person stay engaged and deliver their best.

Are there any barriers or problems I can work on that will help you?
Sometimes, people won't tell you about problems unless you ask. If you can influence or change anything, take note and take action. Let the person know when the issue is solved.

Can I adjust how we work together in any way that would be helpful to you?
Be open. If they think one-on-one meetings are too long, be open to shortening them. If they think a process is burdensome, honestly consider if you can make adjustments. Listen closely and adjust where you can. Some requests may be unrealistic. If they are, it's best to say you will consider it, and follow up with the person after you have had a chance to more fully consider their request or seek coaching help.

Is there anything top-of-mind for you that we haven't talked about?
This leaves the door open for more discussion in case you missed something. It also lets them know how you want to hear from them.

Wrap the meeting by recapping how they are making a difference to the company, the team, and you. Let them know you are grateful for their contributions to the team.

Sabbata-Quit

Not every opportunity works out this way, but if circumstances allow, take time off between your positions to prepare for a strong start in your new management role.

When Madeline changed organizations and took on a management role, she was able to take a sabbatical from her former organization (based on tenure) before she left. This meant she wrapped up work in May, took June off, and began her new role in early July.

She knew she needed a break from work itself, but what she didn't realize was that she also needed a palate cleanse—the chance to reflect and reset. During that month, she picked apart what she wanted to leave behind and what she wanted to bring with her. She determined she was most nervous about building trust with her new team and learning enough about the industry to be an effective leader. In the quiet of her break, she journaled (her best way to process ideas and problems). She reviewed the strengths she exhibited in her previous role and identified which ones would give her a leg up in this job. She asked smart people in her network for advice, and she thought about this new role in the context of her career. All these activities reduced her feelings of nervousness and pressure.

She notes that healthy disconnection is hard to achieve over a long weekend, versus an entire week (or month). The goal is to give yourself enough mental space and time between roles to keep yourself from falling into the same routines and habits you developed in your previous role. Aim to reset your curiosity, your energy, your optimism. Try to catch any habits or biases that might prevent you from excelling. Reflect.

During this time, don't forget to celebrate! You've taken an incredible step. This is a terrific time to connect with friends and do things for yourself to celebrate your progress.

Even if you're moving within the same organization, this strategy is impactful, especially if you are shifting from an individual contributor to a manager. Create the opportunity to reflect. Shifting from a doer mindset to a manager mindset is very tough to accomplish over a weekend, and you will benefit from more time and space. When you arrive on Day One, you need to bring a different view of work, and changing embedded habits takes up valuable brain space and energy. Frankly, you'll need all the mental prowess and energy you can muster during this time to listen, absorb, and ask good questions.

Time off between roles set Madeline up to successfully listen, absorb, and process right away. Taking the time to clear your slate is more than worth it. Make the time, if you can!

Team Retreat

At times, you will have the opportunity to gather your team away from the day-to-day routine. This is a great opportunity for bonding, planning, and innovation.

When Madeline organized a retreat for her team, the primary goal was to build relationships across her team. Her team members worked across three different time zones and had never met in person. This meant their working relationships weren't very deep, and they didn't feel very accountable to each other. To take on the high-level objective, Madeline focused her attention on three aspects to plan the event.

Objectives: Building team relationships was the primary focus, but that isn't something a retreat leader can pop onto an agenda. Madeline defined three areas for her team to work on during the retreat: Team Introductions, What's Good and What's Broken, and Team Values. As the team worked through the activities and exercises she created to focus on each of these goals, they would also meet the overall objective to build and strengthen team relationships.

Materials and agenda: A critical part of the agenda was leaving time for breaks, not only to allow folks to check for urgent emails and take bio breaks, but also to facilitate side get-to-know-you conversations and give introverted members of the team a chance to recharge. Once the breaks and lunch hour were defined, Madeline worked backwards to ensure the topics were distributed with time to build focus and flow from activity to break to activity. With the skeleton of the timeline established, Madeline shifted topics to align with when her group was likely to be energized and engaged: intros first, then discussions about what was working and what wasn't, followed by lunch, then a brainstorming session about the team's overall identity and values. The middle portion of the agenda (focusing on what's good and what's broken) would prompt her team to think about specific instances and examples, which would prime the group to make brainstorming less intimidating and more effective later in the day.

Madeline kept materials simple. She used a template to create and print "trading cards" for her introduction activity which included spaces for items like the team member's time zone, preferred communication method, and tea versus coffee preference. Sticky notes were used to list what was working and what wasn't, and a large notepad let her document the team's responses to her prompts about team values.

Doubters: Madeline knew her group contained more than one person who wouldn't immediately buy into the concept of a retreat. She connected with these team members before the retreat to give them a sneak peek of the agenda and ask for their feedback. By priming them and asking for their thoughts in advance, her doubters better understood her rationale and end goals. To Madeline's delight, this prep paid off. Her doubters contributed throughout the day and in multiple activities.

Since the event was scheduled in mid-December, the retreat wrapped up with a gingerbread house decorating contest. Each small group's entry was scored by three leaders in the department. As Madeline watched, her team frosted and sprinkled while fiercely talking smack to the other teams. One of her senior leaders pulled her aside and noted she'd never seen a particular team member engage with his peers like this, with enthusiasm and energy. By spending time facilitating deeper introductions between her people, then asking them to identify successes and problems, and concluding with a brainstorming session centered around team values, Madeline had the team working together to solve their own problems. In turn, these activities led to deeper relationships between team members.

Status Reporting

Leaders at all levels are expected to report on the status of their team's work, usually to their bosses or the company board. In many cases, these reports can be read by members of the team, key partners in the projects, and leaders who want to understand the health and impact of the work underway.

Here is counsel for successfully reporting progress and escalating issues:

Most importantly, establish rules for **status colors**. Most status reports include some indicator of "work health," and the most common color scheme is red, yellow, green, with green indicating good health. Define your colors clearly so everyone's yellow, for instance, means the same thing. It is human nature for most to report optimistically and positively. Help your team be consistent and objective. Below are suggested definitions for each color:

GREEN	**For projects:** Recent work is on schedule and the end date is still achievable. Both must be true to be green. If the project was yellow before, we have completed a recent milestone on time and have recovered confidence in our end date. **For sales, manufacturing, and other types of work:** The percentage achieved has us on track to finish the quarter at or above the target.
YELLOW	**For projects:** The most recent milestone (an interim deliverable) was missed and/or there is emerging concern about the project completing on time. Essentially: off track with a plan. **For sales, manufacturing, and other types of work:** The percentage complete or another key measure is not on track to hit the end-of-quarter goal, but we have a plan to recover and expect an update next week.
RED	**For projects:** Two or more milestones were missed in a row (it doesn't matter how early in the project this is, these misses raise questions about our ability to estimate and plan). The end date is at risk, and we likely need help to escalate. Essentially: off track without a plan, or with an incomplete plan. **For sales, manufacturing, and other types of work:** The percentage complete or another key measure is not on track to hit the end-of-quarter goal. We are predicting a miss, or unlikely odds for recovery. (It's worth noting that, at times, a red status can occur because of things outside of our control.)

If the team identifies a yellow or red status, the first line in their notes needs to address the **"path to green"** or plan to recovery. If the issue just arose, the line should include when the team will gather to begin working on recovery.

Create a **standard template** to gather status. This makes it easier to share the updates with others, and they will learn where to look for information.

Be brief and specific. Try like all heck to keep an update to one page. A lot of time is lost in administration of status reporting. Be rigorous about yours. Don't add fields to the report unless they are absolutely necessary. Only report when needed. For example, if software development teams are running Agile two-week code development sprints, they should only report after retrospectives, every two weeks. There is no utility in a weekly report for teams who have two-week clusters of work.

For **email, use the three-inch rule and a clear subject line.** The logic of the three-inch rule is to put your most critical information at the very top of your email, in case the reader never scrolls past the initial screen. Your subject should be clearly stated, and if escalation or urgency is needed, it should be included in the subject line.

Clearly ask for help. Consider what you want your audience to do with the information you're presenting. Do you need help or escalation? If so, be specific. Are you raising awareness of a risk? Ask your team this question when you are working together on status reporting. If you are communicating for awareness, note that no escalation is needed at this time.

Mentoring Cohort Program

Just like you, your team can also benefit from finding people to offer advice and support. A simple way to create a mentoring program inside your company is to offer short-term rotational cohorts.

Begin with a survey. Ask those who are interested in having a mentor to answer a few simple questions:

1. Name, job description, where they work within the organization, their senior leader.

2. Ask them to identify what goal or challenge they want to focus on for the next four months. (Perhaps their need is learning a new coding language, or presenting in front of senior team members, or navigating a new role.)

To **engage leaders**, and drive their accountability for developing staff, you incorporate them into the match process. First, collect all the responses and sort them by senior leader. You can then approach each senior leader and present a list that identifies which folks in their organization need help with a particular issue over the next four months. The leader can then identify people in the company who are best suited to address each mentee's challenge. As the leaders match mentee need to mentors, the leaders learn more about their teams and have a stake in the success of the pairing.

Send a message to these nominated mentors, letting them know senior leadership values their acumen and believes their insights will help others. Are they willing to give 30 to 45 minutes each month for the next four months to support the mentee's challenge?

The mentee will book the meetings and send agendas in advance. All the mentor needs to do is show up, be empathetic, and deliver smart insights. (Given the minimal time commitment, it's rare for anyone to decline.)

Now, you have leaders accountable for developing their people and mentors appropriately matched—and flattered they were asked.

Next, **introduce the mentors to mentees** sharing the challenge mentioned in the survey. Remind them of the duration for the cohort, and ask the mentee to schedule meetings and provide agendas.

You could hold a mentoring cohort kick-off meeting or create an instant messaging group channel to create an additional source of support from other mentees in the cohort. Survey the group at a midpoint (to remind the pairs to connect and to make sure assignments are working well), and celebrate the cohort's completion when the period ends.

In-house cohorts are an affordable, light-weight way to help team members find resources to support their development, share appreciation for senior members, hold leaders accountable, and solve current challenges for staff. Ideally, staff will continue to sign up for each round of cohorts if they have a new area of focus or challenge, building their network and knowledge with each pairing.

Pulse Surveys

Pulse surveys are used to get rapid, point-in-time feedback from employees about their engagement. Your response is essential to your team's engagement.

Pulse surveys vary from organization to organization. If they are used, they are generally brief, recur with frequency, and are used as a quick check of the organization's health, much like a nurse takes a patient's pulse to quickly assess them. Sometimes these surveys only have one question like, "How happy are you to work here?" In other cases, they contain multiple questions about whether someone would recommend the company to friends, if their work seems aligned to strategy, or if their boss supports them and the team, as a whole.

If your organization uses pulse surveys and doesn't have a process for managers, here are steps to consider:

Review and prep
- Get your team's results. Read them all the way through.
- Get a broad sense of the results. Did they go up? Decrease? Hold steady?
- Did anything surprise you?
- Is there something obvious you need to take action on or work to improve?
- Did anything make you mad? If so, talk to someone you trust and work through your feelings before you talk with the team. You just received a gift—tough insight you can work to solve. It's okay to feel down or frustrated about it, and it is your responsibility to show your team your own ability to be professional, humble, and willing to change for the better.
- Look for themes. This is important! When reading through comments and taking notes, do you notice any themes? If a question receives one negative comment, that is an outlier and you shouldn't necessarily take action. Let's say someone comments that team meetings are too long and too structured. What if the other

35 people on the team appreciate the meetings? If you change the meeting for one grouchy person, you are undoing a resource for others. Not every complaint needs a response. Outliers can be both bad AND good. A comment might say, "You are an amazing leader," while six other comments generally talk about how strategy is unclear and it is impacting the team. Don't be distracted by your one cheerleader when there are clusters of comments that indicate you need to improve.

Share with team and plan actions
- Before a team meeting, send the results to the group.
- Schedule a workshop meeting and send an agenda. It should include a quick recap of the results, in addition to questions you want to put to the team, including:
  - Of the positives in the survey, what do you think we can do to build on strengths?
  - Of the negatives in the survey, is there anything I can do as a manager, or we can do as a team, to improve?
- During the meeting, open with a quick recap and actively listen to your team as they talk about the positives and negatives.
- Take notes and play back what you hear. For example, "It sounds like we are saying that increased communication could help us better navigate the transition to Agile development."
- Set action items and owners.
- Follow up (so important!).
- Complete your action items.
- Follow up with the team in the near future to check on progress.
- Celebrate your next pulse survey results as numbers improve.

If You Are Undermined

When you become a new manager, you are especially vulnerable to people undermining you. This is very nuanced and complicated, but surmountable.

There are different scenarios in which undermining can happen. In some cases, you might be left off a meeting invitation. Someone might take credit for your idea or gossip about a mistake you made to others. My least favorite is when someone acts positive or neutral in person, but calls you out in front of others when they believe there are errors in your approach.

Years ago, I had figured out how to solve a complex problem about scheduling technical software releases. I was only a few months into my role, and I was so excited about the potential break-through. It was a great way to show my value, especially since I was a nontra-ditional hire for this company. I took my proposal to a group of leaders, and Tom eviscerated me in the meeting. He announced to the group, "This is the problem when people with no industry experience are hired." He threw his notes down on the table and said I clearly needed to go back and rework this because my idea would never work.

I fought tears as I left the room. I felt confident about my idea, but this guy had basically called me stupid in front of the leadership team.

Let's talk about what happens when people undermine others:

First, and most importantly, recognize that the person doing the undermining is pressing on a vulnerability you have: perhaps your lack of knowledge (about the business, project, team, leadership dynamics), your self-doubt, or your inability to move quickly as you learn. Tom took advantage of my lack of deep familiarity with the business to make it look like my analysis was incomplete, and he leveraged his very long tenure to sway the group his way.

Secondly, people undermine for a reason. Try to figure out what is behind the behavior. Were they passed over for the role you have now? Did they advocate for a person with a business background, and you have a technical background? Is there a new CEO, and they seem to be using this chance to make you look bad to elevate themselves? There is a reason they are behaving this way. They have some reason to discredit you. When you understand it, you can start to address the real issue. Tom, I later learned, didn't have a college degree. He started at the lowest level in the company and worked up to leadership. He had deep pride in his understanding of the company. Normally, when someone came up from junior levels, they sought him out for counsel. I came into the company with strong experience, and I hadn't done that. He firmly believed people had to work their way up, and to his mind, I hadn't shown respect for his history, and I hadn't earned the right to recommend solutions.

I was mad, honestly. But I took a deep breath (actually a lot) and sent him a note. I asked if he would be willing to meet with me once a week to help with questions I had. I told him the meeting helped me realize how critical it was to vet my approaches with the operations team. I knew how precious his time was, but would he be willing to mentor me?

He responded well, and we started meeting on Thursday mornings. I would bring questions and listen carefully to his guidance. Over time, I started bringing questions or ideas about my work to him. When I presented the idea for improving deployments again about five weeks later, he was in full support. Tom announced to the group that he wanted to compliment me on the depth of research I had done (also a reflection of the insight he had shared with me during our meetings).

I wish I could tell you he just had an ego, and that when I was deferential, he was supportive. The truth is, I learned a lot from him. I needed him, and he needed to know that I needed him. He became a supporter. It was a good adjustment for me, though honestly, pretty hard to make.

When you are new to a role, you are learning your team, your business, and the human dynamics of your company. Usually, being undermined can come as a surprise, and it can be frustrating.

Another time, a new chief technology officer joined my company. One of my peers sent him a long recommendation about how we should do strategic planning differently. The catch? Strategic planning was my responsibility, not his. I wasn't copied on the email, and he hadn't talked to me. When I was invited to a meeting to discuss it, I was surprised to hear my processes being critiqued. In the meeting, I hid my anger and listened. I then noted that this was the first time I was hearing about these ideas, and I was glad we were discussing them as a group (a cleaned-up version of what I was really thinking!). The CTO figured out pretty quickly what was going on and recommended we stay the course with the existing process for now, but consider changes in the future.

I came out of that discussion wiser. Now I knew this fellow was undercutting me. As I thought about it, I realized he was angling for a promotion with the new leader. It wasn't something personal about me; this guy was fighting for a new role. When I started observing carefully, I realized he was doing the same thing to other people.

When I began to adjust the processes a few months later, he was the first person I reached out to. I told him I thought it would help me validate the changes if he and his team could consider the impact and effectiveness. By getting him on my side, I had support for the changes I eventually recommended.

You can take away three useful pieces of advice from these stories:

1. **Get dissenters in the boat.**
    Remember that saying: "No one drills a hole in a boat they are sitting in." If you want people to stop drilling holes in your boat, get them in the boat with you. Ask them to guide you. Take them early versions of your ideas. In time, these will become their ideas too, and they will do anything to make sure the boat stays afloat. In both these stories, I coaxed my detractors into the boat with me.

2. **Don't let people know when they throw you off balance.** If you are ambushed by undermining during a meeting or conversation, use the phrase, "This is the first time I am hearing about this. I'd like to take some time to consider this and follow up." Hold firm. Don't get rushed into a bad decision or commitment. Don't respond in the moment. Keep your composure.

3. **Opt for in-person meetings.** This last piece of advice came from one of my favorite mentors. She said it is impossible for most people to behave badly when they are face-to-face with someone. She encouraged me to go see someone personally when I was frustrated. No online messages, no talking to other people. Meet in person, if you can. Her point was, it is hard to hold on to anger when you are together. If you think about it, if you are angry and have the chance to send an anonymous message, that message will likely be worded differently than if your name and contact information were attached. When we are a named responder, or respond in person, we think about the longer context of working with someone. We measure our words. We are carefully accurate. We can see when someone gets upset and adjust our language.

Here is the quick advice list for when you are undermined:

1. Don't react in the moment, keep your composure, defer, and collect your thoughts if you can.

2. Try to figure out why the person is doing it. They likely have something to gain from their behavior. If you understand this, you can react.

3. Get them in the boat with you.

4. Go face-to-face. Pay attention to your observations.

Dealing with undermining behavior is complicated, but in almost all cases, you can work through it.

Managing During Change and Crisis

Pandemics. Reorganizations. Layoffs. Even something positive, like a top leader departing to take on a new opportunity, creates unplanned change and worry. Crisis comes in many forms. During these times, managers matter more than ever.

If you are familiar with change models, they all show that **humans react in consistent ways to change. Every time.** No matter how prepared they think they are. First, they are shocked. Then, anxiety rises and morale decreases. Ultimately, they recover as they learn more and figure out how to deal with change. There is no avoiding this pattern.

Let's look at a fully negative change, like the unexpected death of your start-up company's founder. The company is at a fragile point, preparing to fund its next stage. You are deeply concerned, and your team is as well. Many of you were close to the founder, so you are mourning while you're also worried about keeping your jobs and maintaining the financial stability of the company.

In this case, though it's critical to be flexible, you'll still want to take a few moments to map your steps:

1. First, gather your team in a huddle (in-person, if possible). Tell them of Jason's passing and share your own sorrow. As critically, share your confidence in the legacy of the leader. You can say something like, "Jason's vision is clear, and we have support from our board and investors. We will share more as we learn details. Right now, let's take care of each other and hug our loved ones."

2. As the management team gathers, you and your peers will identify critical short-term actions to keep the company stabilized. You can share part of what you discuss, but part may be kept in confidence. Summarize the critical steps you will share with your teams in writing.

3. Share stabilization steps with lower-level managers and let them ask questions. They can then share the steps with their team members.

4. Perhaps add a weekly team meeting. Let people know you are doing this to let them talk and so you can share whatever information you can. Keep yourself strong and forward-looking.

5. Pay particular attention to people on your team who are especially impacted—Jason's college roommate who is the team lead for a group of your folks, for example.

6. Continue to work with leaders to provide frequent updates to the team, even if your only update is, "Nothing new has emerged this week."

Sometimes, the crisis involves a big change that is largely positive, but will greatly impact the team.

Let's say Shondra works on your team and is an excellent performer. Her reputation spreads, and another team approaches you to ask if she would be a good candidate to promote into a leadership role for their team. Honestly, at first you feel nauseous. She is your team's top person. She carries the hardest project, and everyone loves her. You call your partner on the way home from the office and talk about how this would mess up long-term plans you have for your team. But you know this is best for Shondra. You get a good night's sleep (or a few) and take a deep breath. You do the right thing for her and the company.

You help her prepare for the internal interview, and in doing so, you start to think about what you are going to have to change if she gets the job. The interview process takes three weeks. Over that time, you figure out that a key part of her primary project wraps up in the next few days. If you break the remaining work into two parts, you can have junior people cover it. You also realize she plays a key role in mentoring one of your new college graduates, and they have a close relationship. If she earns the promotion, she likely won't have time to mentor him. You reach out to the head of Talent and Development to see about adding the young man to a mentoring cohort next month.

By the time Shondra is offered the job, you have figured out how you will manage without her. You feel calm because you had time to get upset, then figure out the answers.

When your team and her project team hear the news, they will have that same nauseous feeling you did four weeks ago. Even though your plan feels solid to you, you will need to slow down and share your approach with everyone else so the team's performance doesn't suffer. An empathy gap is created as you feel ready, and they feel surprised. Developing a

communications schedule can help you lead change. Here is how it could look in this situation:

1. List all the people you need to inform about the change, and figure out who should find out first.

2. Write a schedule with defined times. At 3:00 p.m., we send this. At 3:15, we meet with this group. At 3:30, this email goes to everyone. It may feel over defined, but it helps you manage the message and make sure folks feel included and considered.

    a. Talk to Shondra beforehand about how to manage messaging. Determine how much of the interviewing should be done in confidence, and talk about how it will help her professional image within the company to develop careful communications plans. Share the potential plans with her.

    b. Depending on her seniority and the criticality of her project, you may need to let senior members of the organization know of the possible change in advance, and how you plan to adapt work and responsibilities. If you tell them in advance, ask them to keep the information in confidence until an announcement is made.

    c. Most importantly, since Shondra is leaving her project, that team should be told first and in private. If you know who will take over her work, share that information. If not, share when you expect to give an update. This provides the team a chance to process the news, ask questions, and be ready when others ask questions. You set the tone for a confident transition, as opposed to one governed by anxiety or worry.

d. Knowing that word will spread quickly, you should immediately let Shondra's new team know the news. Have an email ready to send, or have a quick huddle scheduled with the group. In your plan, prepare notes with key messages so you cover the important points. Perhaps you want to reinforce the company's commitment to internal talent pipelines, your confidence in Shondra and her work results, and how you are confident in the team's ability to build on what Shondra started and to deliver well.

e. The other groups she supports and works with need to be informed next, and they will need to know how this move will impact them. Share your plans for covering her work. Reinforce key messages.

f. Lastly, release an organization-wide announcement that

shares the news, congratulates Shondra on her new role, reinforces the company values she embodies, shares how her success in previous roles led to this point, and (if appropriate for the full audience) articulates how her work will be transitioned.

Fully considering the people who will be impacted, and how you will be sensitive to them, is critical.

As you look at these two scenarios, you can see similarities. Here are the top ways to lead during a crisis:

1. **Promise you will share information when you can, and then do it.** Notice "when you can" in the sentence above. You will be told details (the percentage of staff that will be laid off, the departure date of a key leader) that you cannot relay to your team. But some things you can and should share, and share quickly.

    If you learn something, consider gathering your team together within the hour for a quick 15-minute touchbase. Tell them what you know, and whether to expect a news story or follow-up announcement from the company. Make sure they don't find out about something important from someone else or from external sources.

    Give them your perspective and give them hope. If someone is leaving, share your thoughts on why the person was impactful to the company. Tell them how excited you are about the new person who is coming in. If details of a challenge are still emerging, remind them about how the team can pull together to navigate changes ahead.

2. **If you don't have an answer, say, "I don't know, and I promise to share when I can."**

3. **Don't cancel team meetings or one-on-ones.** People need consistency to balance ambiguity or disruption. Even if it feels hard for you, keep team meetings going so folks have time to connect with each other and you.

4. **If you make changes, explain why.** Perhaps you delay the release of your team's OKRs (Objectives and Key Results quarterly plan) because you want to be sure the new leader has a chance to weigh in. Share that with the team. The stories people make up in their minds are usually worse than the truth. Share the story.

5. **Listen. Watch. Make time. Be aware.** Your number one job is to keep people calm during the crisis. To do that, you have to understand what they need. Do they need you to listen? Are they looking to you for confidence about a future outcome? Do they need comfort? Slow down. Be present and invest time in your team.

6. **Set timelines and stages for communications.** Much like the example of Shondra's promotion, when there is a change, consider doing the following:

a. Determine which people you need to inform, and figure out who should know first.

b. Write a schedule. Define the times. Use the guidelines from the prior section about Shondra's promotion.

c. Make a list of who in the group you are informing will find out first, who needs to keep confidentiality, and the update method (Quick face-to-face huddle? Email? Announcement in a larger meeting?). Think through who will be impacted. Make sure to think about how this will impact them, and address areas of concern (or let them know when you will be updating).

Consistency and steadiness from you, frequent communication about what is happening, and a detailed plan will help your team navigate the turbulent days of change.

17

You've Got This and We Have You

Keep being an opportunist. Pay attention to things that work well, and do them more often. Pay attention to what doesn't work. Adjust.

Good managers learn how to be managers. Great managers keep learning. When we were writing this book, Madeline told me how she runs her team meetings, and I realized she has great best practices. So, I leveraged her ideas and incorporated them into my meetings the following week.

Keep being an opportunist. Pay attention to things that work well, and do them more often. Pay attention to what doesn't work. Adjust.

At the end of Madeline's first year, she was dealing with a large program crisis while we were working on this book. We met at a small restaurant a short walk from her office. It's one of her favorite places. There's a fireplace and windows framed by velvet curtains that look onto a bustling sidewalk. We settled into mismatched chairs at a little table by the window, and just sat for a few minutes, drinking our tea and watching the world move by.

She said, "I'm failing. I can't seem to catch up or solve the newest program issue." I said, "Tell me more," and she started to recount what was happening.

A peer manager needed her best practices for onboarding new clients, and she needed to send those off.

The Business Development team was frustrated that they couldn't find time to talk about the new contract structure Madeline had recommended to reduce administrative overhead (and also increase their profit margins on the project).

A former team member needed Madeline's best practices for setting up team meetings.

While her new hire was doing wonderfully, another team wanted to poach one of her top performers.

Accounting needed progress updates for the current contract, so they could get the billing out.

She had an idea related to her big program, but realized it would be something different than had ever been done before, and she was thinking about how to get others on board with the idea.

I sat for a moment and then had a realization. I asked if I could play back what she had just said. She agreed.

I said, I think you just told me:

Even though you have only been in the role a year, another team wants to use your onboarding best practices. The Business Development team loves your ideas on contract structure because it drives margins up, and they are motivated to talk about it. The struggling person whom you coached into a new role thinks so highly of your team members that she wants to use them in her new team; you have become known as such a strong talent finder and developer that people are trying to steal your folks. And, maybe most importantly, the client who was so unhappy when you started is now paying their bills on time, and you already have a plan to solve the program problems?

I stopped and watched her expression changed. We both laughed.

I told her, "Madeline, that's a hell of a first year. Don't let today's to-do list force you to miss all you've accomplished."

This role of people manager is its own vertical area of expertise. Lean on this guide. Lean on others. Have faith in yourself. You will build the muscle. And slow down, have a tea, and let your mentor remind you of all you have accomplished when you are one year in.

You've got this.

TOOLS INDEX
Worksheets

(These are checklists with prompts to help the new manager complete a successful conversation, workshop, research, plan).

Want to work with Christine?

Christine Sandman Stone is a trusted advisor to organizations and leaders and a mentor to hundreds of working professionals. She has a reputation for solving big problems with practical, efficient solutions.

To inquire about her speaking engagements and services–including strategic planning, assessments, coaching, and workshops–visit **www.christinesandmanstone.com** or e-mail **christine@deliveratscale.com**.